WHERE THE SPIRIT LEADS

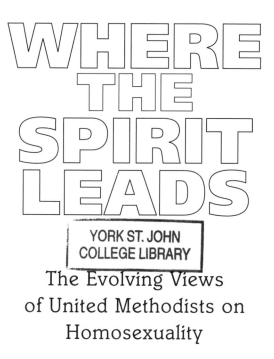

WHERE THE SPIRIT LEADS

The Evolving Views
of United Methodists on
Homosexuality

James Rutland Wood

ABINGDON PRESS
Nashville

WHERE THE SPIRIT LEADS
THE EVOLVING VIEWS OF UNITED METHODISTS ON HOMOSEXUALITY

Copyright © 2000 by Abingdon Press

This book is printed on acid-free paper.

Library of Congress Cataloging-in-Publication Data

Wood, James R., 1933-
    Where the Spirit leads : the evolving views of United Methodists on homosexuality / James Rutland Wood.
        p. cm.
    Includes bibliographical references.
    ISBN 0-687-08217-X (alk. paper)
    1. Homosexuality—Religious aspects—United Methodist Church (U.S.)
    2. United Methodist Church (U.S.)—Doctrines. I. Title.

    BX8385.H6 W66 2000
    261.8'35766'08827 21—dc21
                                                                    99-041271

All scripture quotations unless noted otherwise are taken from the *New Revised Standard Version,* copyright © 1989, the Division of Christian Education of the National Council of the Churches of Christ in the United States of America. Used by permission. All rights reserved.

Scripture quotations noted NEB are from *The New English Bible.* © The Delegates of the Oxford University Press and The Syndics of the Cambridge University Press 1961, 1970. Reprinted by permission.

Selections from *Daily Christian Advocate, Advance Edition* © 1996 by The United Methodist Publishing House. Used by permission.

Selections from *Daily Christian Advocate, Volume III* © 1996 by The United Methodist Publishing House. Used by permission.

Selections from *The Book of Discipline of The United Methodist Church,* © 1996 by The United Methodist Publishing House. Used by permission.

00 01 02 03 04 05 06 07 08 09—10 9 8 7 6 5 4 3 2 1

MANUFACTURED IN THE UNITED STATES OF AMERICA

In loving memory of
"Granfannie" whose heart
was as my heart

CONTENTS

INTRODUCTION
Sleeping or Watching?

Washington Irving's fictional account of Rip Van Winkle, who slept through the American Revolution, dramatically depicts the changes that took place in a short span of history. But we can learn another lesson from the story: Because he was sleeping, Rip Van Winkle played no role in shaping those changes.

The Wake-Up Call

God is calling United Methodists to wake up and shape the course of history. To be sure, neither the Bible nor history allows us to believe that God's purposes stand or fall on what Methodists do. Yet both the Bible and history attest that God is at work in the world, calling human instruments for divine purposes. This book asserts that God is calling The United Methodist Church (UMC) to a mission for which it is uniquely suited: to lead contemporary people and societies to a culturally aware biblical faith.

> God is Calling United Methodists to shape the course of history.

United Methodists are biblical Christians. Through the Bible, and especially through its "story of Jesus," we know the love, justice, mercy, and saving power of God. As culturally aware biblical Christians we affirm the authority of the Bible while interpreting the Bible in the light of the culture of its authors. And we watch for the living word that the God of the Bible speaks to each of us in our own culture. Fulfilling our mission will shape the way people access the Bible and gain its power; the way the Bible informs public policy; and, specifically, the way people and societies accept gay and lesbian persons.

The basic argument of this book applies to The United Methodist Church worldwide. God's call is to the global church. Moreover, precisely because we are a global connection, one part of the church can never resolve an issue in isolation. Nevertheless, for three reasons I have addressed this book primarily to United Methodists in the United States. First, the crisis over homosexuality in the church is urgent in the United States. Second, despite the urgency, I will argue in chapter 7 that the climate for resolving the issue now is favorable in the United States. The third reason I have addressed this book primarily to United Methodists in the United States is that the primary empirical basis of its argument is my survey of U.S. delegates to the 1996 General Conference, supplemented by United Methodists' responses to a series of polls of the U.S. population.

Facing Our Crisis

> Our crisis endangers our ability to answer God's call.

Because answering God's call both requires and facilitates the unity of the UMC, we must face squarely our present crisis. Our crisis poses a danger to the unity of the UMC, to the persistence of Methodism, and, therefore, to our ability to answer God's call. In fact, some vocal critics of the UMC believe our present crisis over homosexuality foreshadows our demise.

Many see the issue of homosexuality as the core of United Methodism's crisis. I find it more helpful to see homosexuality as one manifestation of a much deeper crisis over interpreting the Bible and receiving its power. The issues over homosexuality will not be fully resolved until all are assured that the resolution upholds the authority of the Bible and opens the church to the power of the God of the Bible. Chapter 1, "Seeing Our Differences," describes and assesses United Methodism's crisis.

We must face our crisis, but we should do so with full knowledge that the heritage that unites us is stronger than the issues that divide us. Chapter 2, "Claiming Our Heritage," explores some of the central themes of our Methodist heritage: biblical religion that is experienced, openness to theological and social diversity, geographical and social outreach, connectionalism, and social action as an expression of biblical faith.

Four Christian Imperatives

The book alerts leaders at all levels of the church to four interrelated Christian imperatives. Heeding these imperatives will help us resolve our differences as we advance our mission.

• We must engage each other in a biblical dialogue about our differences! When discussions about contested issues become conversations about the Bible a way is opened for their resolution. Chapter 3, "Talking About the Bible," elaborates this theme, examining controversies in the New Testament church and explaining what it means to have a *culturally aware* biblical faith.

• We must love God with our minds! This clear biblical mandate is essential if we are to apply the gospel to our culture. Yet it is often slighted when controversial issues evoke an ideological response. The fourth chapter, "Opening Our Minds," discusses how this imperative relates to our understanding of the Bible and to our discernment of God's revelations to our own culture.

• We must enlarge our networks of personal relationships! The gospel compels us to widen our circles of caring and concern; as we do, we often find our ideas and behavior profoundly changed. Chapter 5, "Enlarging Our Circles," shows how enlarging our circles influences our thought in ways that open our lives to the Holy Spirit.

• We must honor our mutual agreements! The UMC has a sound process for negotiating agreements; but that process, and the church itself, are jeopardized when any of us fail to honor these agreements. The sixth chapter, "Honoring Our Agreements," treats this topic, including how we keep our disagreements from impeding our mission.

As we heed these biblically based imperatives, we will already have begun to model a vital, culturally aware biblical faith; and we will gain knowledge and power for answering God's call.

I interpret these imperatives in the light of my thirty-five years of studying church leaders in the midst of controversy. Most recently my studies have included a survey of 1996 General Conference delegates and observations of the Theological Diversity Dialogues in Nashville and Dallas as well as the Council of Bishops meetings in Lincoln, Nebraska; Norcross, Georgia; and Chattanooga, Tennessee; and the Connectional Process Team in Charlotte, North Carolina.

Watching with the Holy Spirit

The final chapter, "A Time to Lead," summarizes and elaborates my argument that God is calling the UMC to lead contemporary people and societies to a culturally aware biblical faith. This chapter also describes my vision of how, watching with the Holy Spirit, we will resolve our crisis and answer God's call through acting out our faith.

A Survey of General Conference Delegates

As the argument unfolds, I will refer frequently to my survey of U.S. delegates to the 1996 meeting of the General Conference—the lawmaking body for the UMC. Seventy percent of those delegates (589) returned completed questionnaires. Though the delegates I surveyed are only a fraction of the members of The United Methodist Church, their views are especially important for several reasons. First, they are persons who have been elected by their annual conferences, hence they have inspired the confidence of their peers within the church and may be considered as persons whose views will be given serious consideration by those peers. Second, from delegates' views we can make some inferences about the probability of various actions by the General Conference as it makes laws and sets policies for the general church. Third, though delegates to the General Conference may have views significantly different from the views of the people they represent, delegates likely represent the views that the members in general would hold were they to have the same opportunity to become fully informed and to discuss issues with others.[1] In fact, we will see that, on some issues central to our crisis, the views of the general population of United Methodists in the U.S. are changing rapidly.

United Methodists in National Surveys

Where possible, I have supplemented my data on General Conference delegates with data from national polls, especially the General Social Survey (GSS). The GSS is a biennial series of U.S. population polls conducted by the National Opinion Research Center at the University of Chicago.[2] Since the GSS provides data by denomination, I could obtain the responses of United Methodists. There are usually between seventy-five and two hundred United Methodists in each poll. I generally combine two polls (for example 1996 and 1998) so that there will be at least one hundred respondents.

Acknowledgments

Many people and several institutions have contributed ideas, encouragement, and other resources to this project. I wish to thank the Lilly Endowment and The Louisville Institute for support of my attendance at the 1992 and 1996 General Conferences and the surveys of delegates to those conferences. I also wish to thank the Organizing Religious Work project at Hartford Seminary for support of my observations of the Theological Diversity Dialogues, a Council of Bishops meeting, and a meeting of the Connectional Process Team. Individuals who gave helpful ideas or advice as social scientists or in other academic roles include Dr. Nancy Ammerman, Dr. John Bancroft, Dr. Alan Bell, Dr. Craig Dykstra, Dr. Paul Gebhard, Dr. David James, Dr. Jeanne Knoerle, Dr. James Lewis, Dr. David Roozen, Dr. Collin Williams, and Dr. Martin Weinberg. Before I list several participants and observers of the UMC from whom I learned most, I must acknowledge that most of them would likely want to distance themselves from some of the ideas in the book and some see a quite different vision than the one I describe in chapter 7. With this caveat, I wish to thank Dr. Ernest Davidson, Dr. Victor Paul Furnish, the Reverend James Heidinger, II, Bishop Leroy Hodapp, Bishop Rueben Job, Bishop David J. Lawson, Dr. David Lundquist, Dr. Kent Millard, the Reverend Mary Ann Moman, the Reverend David Owen, Dr. Russell Richey, the Reverend Richard Ruach, Mr. William Smith, Dr. Scott Thumma, Dr. Philip Wogaman, and Bishop Joseph Yeakel. As always, my wife, Myriam

Revel Wood, has been my companion, inspiration, and intellectual gadfly throughout this project.

My largest debt is to the 589 delegates to the 1996 General Conference whose thoughtful responses to my questions inspired me to write a different kind of book from the one I originally had in mind.

The spirit of this book reflects my reading of W. E. Sangster's *Methodism Can Be Born Again*, published by The Methodist Book Concern in 1938. Sangster challenges "the people called Methodists" to reform their bloated and ineffective organization and to recover early Methodism's sense of fellowship, acceptance of assurance, passion for holiness, and zeal for personal evangelism. Sangster's book is aflame with the biblical faith of Methodism but exudes the spirit of the gospel with no need of proof texts.

This book is dedicated to my grandmother, Frances (Fannie) Watson Rutland, who though she believed that every word of the Bible was truly, literally God's word, never found a word that allowed her to think ill of anyone or to treat anyone as less than a child of God.

CHAPTER ONE
Seeing Our Differences

"METHODISTS MAD AS HELL," screamed the headline of one of the Denver papers. During the 1996 United Methodist Church General Conference, fifteen of our bishops told the press that they disagreed with the United Methodist Church's official position that the practice of "homosexuality is incompatible with Christian teaching" and with the restrictions on homosexuals derived from that position. No General Conference has ever acted to exclude homosexual persons from membership in the church. However, the 1972 General Conference condemned the practice of homosexuality and subsequent General Conferences restricted the UMC's role in "promoting" homosexuality and excluded "self-avowed practicing homosexuals" from ordination and ministry in the church.[1] The fifteen bishops were protesting these restrictions.

> Sincere, articulate, and well-organized elements of the church are at opposite poles on the issue.

The Denver Fifteen

I mean no disrespect with this heading. Some do use the term pejoratively, but others positively associate the action of the fifteen bishops with persons who in the 1960s challenged established ideas and authorities. Representatives of the fifteen bishops called a news conference to issue the following statement. Many of their fellow bishops and most delegates to the General Conference learned about the statement in the newspaper.

We the undersigned bishops wish to affirm the commitment made at our consecration to the vows to uphold the
Discipline of the church. However, we must confess the
pain we feel over our personal convictions that are contra-
dicted by the proscriptions in the *Discipline* against gay
and lesbian persons within our church and from our
ordained and diaconal ministers. Those sections are para-
graphs 71F (last paragraph); 402.2; 906.12; and footnote,
p. 205. We believe it is time to break the silence and state
where we are on this issue that is hurting and silencing
countless faithful Christians. We will continue our responsibility to the order and discipline of the church but urge
United Methodist churches to open the doors in gracious
hospitality to all brothers and sisters in the faith.

We will see that the crisis in United Methodism is much
deeper than the issue of homosexuality, but we cannot
resolve deeper issues until we face up to this one. The
"Denver Fifteen" became the lightning rod for the issue of
homosexuality. The bishops' action triggered intense reac-
tions within the General Conference sessions and by various caucus groups. Some argued that the bishops' action
was necessary to force the denomination both to face the
division among its members on the issue of homosexuality and to prepare it to play a constructive role in the
American society's struggle with this issue. Others insist-
ed that any change in UMC policy on this issue would be
contrary to the Bible and would lead to schism.
Outspoken delegates pressed the Council of Bishops to
make a statement in response to the fifteen bishops. After
long deliberation the Council of Bishops released a short
statement, beginning with the following paragraph:

We, the Council of Bishops of The United Methodist
Church, acknowledge the serious differences that exist
among United Methodists on issues related to homosexuality. These differences are also reflected within the

Council of Bishops. We have been praying together and have been talking with one another in a new spirit of honesty and openness that is both painful and hopeful.[2]

The fifteen bishops forced attention to an issue that many would be happy to ignore. Quite a few delegates took me to task for asking so many questions about homosexuality when the General Conference had so many far-reaching issues. Indeed, when I asked delegates to tell me the most significant action of the conference, few mentioned this issue. They were focused on mission, ministry, and the structural changes that would facilitate them. Many delegates expressed impatience with the time and energy devoted to the issue of homosexuality and wanted somehow to put it behind them. More recently I have observed this impatience with the issue in both the Theological Diversity Dialogues and the April/May 1998 meetings of the UMC Council of Bishops. In the dialogues several participants wanted to make clear that the homosexuality issue is just the current manifestation of differences on interpreting the scriptures. And many of the bishops at the Council of Bishops meeting stressed that the crises in the world should be our real focus as they far overshadow any crisis we may be having over our differences on homosexuality.

I am sympathetic with all those who are impatient in the sense I have described it. Still almost half the delegates reacted positively to the fifteen bishops' statement in part because they see that failure to face the issue could split the church. Sincere, articulate, and well-organized elements of the church are at opposite poles on the issue, and a significant segment of faithful United Methodists say they feel strongly enough about this issue to leave the church if it is not resolved to their satisfaction.

The Controversy over Homosexuality in The United Methodist Church

At the level of official policy, the issue of homosexuality in the UMC is quite different from that in the Southern Baptist Convention (SBC)—the nation's largest Protestant body. For example the SBC has strongly opposed the offering of health benefits to employees' homosexual partners, making this one of the bases of its boycott of the Walt Disney Company. The 1992 UMC General Conference on the other hand strongly supported such rights. Moreover, 92 percent of 1996 delegates agreed that "Homosexuals should not be discriminated against when it comes to employment outside the church."

Yet United Methodists are sharply divided on three aspects of this issue. In the first place, there is the most basic question of acceptance of "the practice of homosexuality." The UMC first took a position on this aspect of the homosexuality issue when the 1972 General Conference adopted a statement recognizing homosexual persons' need for ministry. During the debate over the statement, the following phrase was added: "although we do not condone the practice of homosexuality and consider this practice incompatible with Christian teaching." The 1996 *Discipline* contains this paragraph:

Homosexual persons no less than heterosexual persons are individuals of sacred worth. All persons need the ministry and guidance of the church in their struggles for human fulfillment, as well as the spiritual and emotional care of a fellowship that enables reconciling relationships with God, with others, and with self. Although we do not condone the practice of homosexuality and consider this practice incompatible with Christian teaching, we affirm that God's grace is available to all. We commit ourselves to be in ministry for and with all persons.[3]

Many believe this condemnation of the practice of homosexuality is nothing less than faithfulness to the Scriptures. A sixty-three-year-old delegate who considers himself a conservative expressed this view: "A return to biblical authority is essential, if any solution on this issue is to be [found]. When the authority of Scripture is no longer our starting point, anything can become acceptable—even the practice of homosexuality." Others find biblical authority for a different view. They believe that the Bible is silent on the matter of committed same-sex relationships and that the *Discipline's* condemnation of all homosexual practice goes counter to the basic teachings of Jesus. A fifty-six-year-old delegate who considers herself a moderate says the solution to the homosexuality issue is, "God's Grace/Love/Unconditional Acceptance."

The debate over the "incompatibility" phrase illustrates that General Conference delegates are closely divided. In both 1992 and 1996 delegates were presented with proposals to substitute a statement recognizing that Methodists are not of one mind on this issue. Here is the statement that was approved by a majority (with a margin of one) of the Church and Society legislative committee at the 1996 General Conference:

> We acknowledge with humility that the Church has been unable to arrive at a common mind on the compatibility of homosexual practice with Christian faith. Many consider this practice incompatible with Christian teaching. Others believe it acceptable when practiced in a context of human covenantal faithfulness. The Church seeks further understanding through continued prayer, study, and pastoral experience. In doing so, the Church continues to affirm that God's grace is bestowed on all and that the members of Christ's body are called to be in ministry for and with one another and to the world.[4]

In Denver, as in Louisville, about 60 percent of the delegates voted to retain the "incompatibility phrase." But the debate is sure to continue. In March 1999 the UMC Board of Church and Society voted to ask the 2000 General Conference to substitute the following phrase for the current "incompatibility phrase": "Although faithful Christians disagree on the compatibility of homosexuality with Christian teaching, . . . " The commission on Christian Unity and Interreligious Concerns also endorsed this change in the *Discipline,* but as we will see, at the 1999 sessions of the annual conferences resolutions to retain the "incompatibility phrase" outnumbered those calling for change.[5]

A second, and related, aspect of the issue for United Methodists is that of same-sex unions. For several years prior to the 1996 General Conference some United Methodist pastors were, usually quietly, conducting ceremonies celebrating same-sex unions. As word spread about these ceremonies, some United Methodists were deeply troubled. Pressure mounted to stop such ceremonies on the grounds that they were contradictory to the *Discipline*'s declaration that "the practice of homosexuality. . . [is] incompatible with Christian teaching." Nonetheless, in some annual conferences the climate for such ceremonies was more friendly. Two attempts by annual conferences to allow local congregations or pastors discretion on such unions were the subject of a Judicial Council decision in October 1993. The Legislative Committee of the Minnesota Conference approved a resolution to give "reconciling congregations the right to offer services of blessing and celebration of committed relationships of couples of the same gender." The bishop ruled that the resolution would be out of order because it violated certain provisions of the *Discipline.* In a second case, the Troy Annual Conference approved a resolution distinguishing covenant services from marriage services and stating "that clergy who wish to may participate in a 'Covenant Service,' which is the celebration of a relationship in which God's love is affirmed." Considering these cases the Judicial Council ruled that only the General Conference has the authority to establish the rites and rituals of The United Methodist Church. This ruling set the stage for a debate on the issue at the 1996 General Conference, and several relevant petitions were considered. On the petition that brought the issue to the floor of the Conference, the legislative committee voted 29 to 25 (with 5 abstentions) that such ceremonies should not be conducted. After a lengthy debate, the General Conference, by a vote of 553 to 321, added the following sentence to the Social Principles: "Ceremonies that celebrate homosexual unions shall not be conducted by our ministers and shall not be conducted in our churches."[6]

My survey asked whether homosexual "marriages" should be permitted within the UMC. Twenty-nine percent of the delegates responded affirmatively. However, several delegates made the distinction between "marriages" and "unions." The vote reported above suggests that 37 percent may favor permitting the celebration of homosexual unions.

The third aspect of the homosexuality issue is ordination of practicing homosexuals. Since 1984, the *Discipline* has been clear on this point:

> Since the practice of homosexuality is incompatible with Christian teaching, self-avowed practicing homosexuals are not to be accepted as candidates, ordained as ministers, or appointed to serve in The United Methodist Church.[7]

About a third of the delegates (34 percent) believe that homosexuals should be ordained within the UMC (given the phrasing of the question, this may overstate support

for ordaining *practicing* homosexuals); and many delegates, like the fifteen bishops, are persistent in their calls to
remove all "proscriptions in the *Discipline* against gay and
lesbian persons within our church."

Some delegates, especially conservative ones, feel so
strongly about the homosexual issue that they say they
would leave the UMC if the issue is not resolved in line
with their convictions.

In February 1998 a press release by the respected conservative caucus, Good News, reported that its board members are now beginning to hear questions about "when"
the UMC will be divided rather than "whether" it will be
divided. According to James V. Heidinger, II, president
and publisher of *Good News*, "At every level of the denomination, many UM leaders are using their influence to help
move the church toward the acceptance of homosexual
practice and the approval of same-sex covenants, despite
the consistent actions of the church's past six general conferences." This concern was later highlighted in an issue of
Good News magazine that pictured a sinking *Titantic* and
asked: "Will homosexuality sink the UMC?"[8] Even more
telling is an open letter from the Good News Board of
Directors to the Council of Bishops, which appears to suggest that some division of the UMC is inevitable. Taking
note of "a growing movement within our church to dis-
obey 'for conscience' sake' the *Discipline* of the church,"
the letter calls on the bishops to "deal with this renuncia-
tion of Scripture, Tradition, and our covenant." They
request the bishops both to enforce church standards and
"to work on processes that would allow the orderly with-
drawal of those who, for whatever reason, cannot submit
to the order and discipline of The United Methodist
Church."[9] I find noteworthy Good News's focus on
the possibility of schism because, based on an analysis of
that organization several years ago, I had concluded that

it plays an important role in holding members in the church—by giving voice to their conservative views.

United Methodists and Abortion

Before looking more closely at those delegates who say they would leave the UMC over the homosexuality issue, let us look at United Methodist views on abortion. Though the abortion issue is not as divisive as I had originally expected, it is a source of controversy.

The 1996 delegates overwhelmingly favor the availability of abortion. Seventy-two percent consider themselves pro-choice. Moreover, 87 percent think abortion is justified if the pregnancy resulted from rape, and 95 percent think abortion is justified to keep the mother alive. General Social Survey data from 1996 suggest that these views of delegates are fairly close to those of United Methodists in general. Nationally, 58 percent of United Methodists think a woman should be able to obtain a legal abortion if "the woman wants it for any reason." (This compares to 29 percent of Southern Baptists and 45 percent of the general population.) Ninety percent of United Methodists think an abortion is justified if the pregnancy resulted from rape, and 97 percent think an abortion is justified if "the woman's health is seriously endangered by the pregnancy."

Yet, partly because of the agonizing examination of the abortion issue in the Church and Society Legislative Committee and subsequent discussion within the last few General Conferences, delegates are well aware of the complexity of the abortion issue. On the matter of abortion to prevent the birth of a child with birth defects, for example, just 45 percent of delegates see such an abortion as justified (compared to 79 percent of United Methodists nationally, and 82 percent of the general U.S. population). Few delegates think financial inability to support a child justifies an abortion—15 percent, compared to 60 percent of United Methodists nationally and 47 percent of the U.S. population.

Sensitivity of delegates to the complexity of the abortion issue is reflected in the Social Principles' statement on abortion:

> Our belief in the sanctity of unborn human life makes us reluctant to approve abortion. But we are equally bound to respect the sacredness of the life and well-being of the mother, for whom devastating damage may result from an unacceptable pregnancy. In continuity with past Christian teachings, we recognize tragic conflicts of life with life that may justify abortion, and in such cases we support the legal option of abortion under proper medical procedures. We cannot affirm abortion as an acceptable means of birth control, and we unconditionally reject it as a means of gender selection. We call all Christians to a searching and prayerful inquiry into the sorts of conditions that may warrant abortion. We commit our Church to continue to provide nurturing ministries to those who terminate a pregnancy, to those in the midst of a crisis pregnancy, and to those who give birth.[10]

The adoption of this thoughtful statement is one reason that the abortion issue does not pose the same threat to UMC unity as the issue of homosexuality. About a third of the delegates who responded to my invitation to describe "a common ground position that might lead to a resolution of the abortion issue" referred to this statement, indicating that this present UMC position *is* a common ground position. Remarkably, 33 percent of those who considered themselves pro-choice gave this response, and 30 percent of those who did not consider themselves pro-choice also gave this response.

The abortion issue still has the potential for controversy.

In fact, fifty-four delegates (9 percent of my respondents) say they would leave the UMC if its position on abortion did not reflect their own views. However, the controversy over abortion does not pose the threat to UMC unity posed by the controversy over homosexuality. Only a third as many delegates say they would leave over abortion as over homosexuality. More important, these delegates represent a spectrum of views on the issue—twenty-two of these delegates are pro-choice; thirty-two are not—and both the pro-choice "leavers" and the non–pro-choice "leavers" are distributed widely across the Jurisdictions. My data show a quite different picture of those who say they would leave over the issue of homosexuality.

Who Would Leave Us over the Issue of Homosexuality?

More than one-fourth of U.S. delegates say they feel strongly enough to leave the UMC! Thirteen delegates (about 2 percent of U.S. delegates) say they would leave if the UMC does not become more accepting of homosexual persons. I'll call these the "liberal leavers." Most who would leave (about 25 percent of U.S. delegates), however, are conservatives who sincerely believe the Bible leaves them no options on the issue of homosexuality. These "conservative leavers" say they would leave if the UMC were to bless homosexual unions or ordain practicing homosexuals. In fact, many of them say they would leave if the "incompatible with Christian teaching" phrase were removed from the *Discipline*. Let's take a closer look at these delegates who say they would leave. Who are they? How strong are their ties to the UMC? Do they have leadership resources to go it alone?

Clearly those who would leave, like those who would stay, were not lacking in Christian love for those who disagreed with them. Eighty-seven percent of the conserva-

> Those who would leave, like those who would stay, have Christian love for those who disagree with them.

tive leavers (compared to 83 percent of all delegates and eleven of the thirteen liberal leavers) had cordial conversations with those who disagreed with them on homosexuality. Ninety-seven percent of the conservative leavers (compared to 98 percent of all delegates and twelve of the thirteen liberal leavers) were willing to be friends with those who disagreed about homosexuality.

Though there are few biblical literalists among the UMC delegates, there is a clear difference between "liberal leavers" and "conservative leavers" in the way they interpret the Bible. Six percent of the conservative leavers (compared to 3 percent of all delegates) say the Bible is to be taken literally. None of the liberal leavers are biblical literalists. Ninety percent of the conservative leavers (compared to 67 percent of all delegates) say the Bible is God's word. Four of the thirteen liberal leavers say the Bible is God's word. (I will say more about the biblical stances of the delegates in chapter 3.) Moreover, 49 percent of the conservative leavers (compared to 18 percent of the total sample) say "God's word does not change." None of the thirteen liberal leavers say "God's word does not change." We will see in chapter 3 that one's stance toward the Bible influences one's stance toward issues.

There are important regional differences. The conservatives who would leave are disproportionately from the South. Forty-seven percent are from the Southeastern Jurisdiction and 15 percent from the South Central Jurisdiction. In contrast, only four of the thirteen liberal leavers are from the South. Just over 82 percent of the conservative leavers are concentrated in ten Southern and four contiguous states. In fact, the majority of delegates in several of these annual conferences said they would leave, suggesting the possibility of a major schism in the South. The remaining 18 percent (twenty-six delegates) are spread over fifteen states. Perhaps in their case simply leaving the church as individuals is more likely than trying to split the church. They would have less social support for splitting, and in fact, since the majority (53 percent) of the American people now support the hiring of homosexuals as clergy, these delegates may not even have enough social support to sustain their leaving the church over this issue.[11] On the other hand, of course, they may be involved in social networks that would even support pulling a local congregation from the UMC or, at least, siphoning off a large proportion of a local congregation to form a new independent church. Furthermore if organizations such as Good News were to support those calling for a split, such organizations could provide social support nationally. Almost half (48 percent) of the "conservative leavers" compared to only 17 percent of all delegates attended a Good News meeting at the General Conference.

Sociologist Nancy Ammerman found that Southern Baptists who supported their denomination's turn back toward fundamentalism were likely to be marginal persons in the sense that, for example, they had less education and less income than members in general.[12] Looking at the UMC conservative leavers in this light, I found no evidence that those contemplating leaving are sociologically marginal. It turns out that they are quite similar to the whole sample in education and income. In fact, a larger percent of them have doctorates (27 versus 24 percent) and incomes in the "$75,000 and over family income" brackets (49 percent versus 38 percent). The conservative leavers are also similar to the whole sample in age and in lay/clergy status. But they are more likely to be male (82 percent) than delegates in the total sample (59 percent). By contrast, eleven of the thirteen liberal leavers are women.

> Those contemplating leaving are not marginal persons.

Finally, the conservative leavers are conservative overall,

not just on the homosexuality issue. Seventy-nine percent (compared to 34 percent of the whole sample) rate themselves conservative on social and political matters. Ninety percent (compared to 40 percent of the total sample) rate themselves conservative on religious matters. Twenty-seven percent (compared to 9 percent of the total sample) would also leave the church over the abortion issue.

A Crisis for Methodism

The United Methodist Reporter quoted a speaker who seems to have given up hope for the UMC: "God may be ready for The United Methodist Church to wither up and blow away."[13] I agree on one point: We can never presume that God will stick with a specific institution. As the biblical scholar H. H. Rowley has forcefully argued: "In the thought of the Old Testament it is always election to service, and it is held to be forfeited when it has no relation to that service."[14] All institutional structures must be watched over carefully. Methodism is more important than the UMC. We do not want the UMC to survive at the expense of Methodism's distinctive virtue. What is the distinctive virtue of Methodism? According to Wesley, Methodists do believe "that all Scripture is given by the inspiration of God...the written Word of God to be the only and sufficient rule both of Christian faith and practice....Christ to be the eternal supreme God."[15] Yet Wesley took an open approach to the interpretation of the Scriptures. Wesley wrote to one congregation, "The Methodists alone do not insist on your holding this or that opinion; but they think and let think."[16]

Even today the willingness to allow whatever opinion about Baptism or the Lord's Supper—including whether or not to baptize or to celebrate the Lord's Supper—is remarkable. And it shows a willingness to interpret the

Scriptures rather freely. When setting forth his understanding of the faith rather than reacting defensively to his
critics, Wesley, like the apostle Paul, could state the essentials of Christianity quite simply:

> Art thou employed in doing, "not thy own will, but the
> will of Him that sent thee?" "Is thy heart right toward thy
> neighbour? Dost thou love, as thyself, all mankind without
> exception?"
>
> Do you show your love by your works? While you have
> time, as you have opportunity, do you in fact "do good to
> all men," neighbours or strangers, friends or enemies,
> good or bad? Do you do them all the good you can;
> endeavouring to supply all their wants; assisting them
> both in body and soul, to the uttermost of your power?[17]

When there is accord on these fundamentals, then there
can be tolerance of great diversity in other matters. And
more than tolerance. Wesley appealed to those who disagreed with him: "Then love me with a very tender affec-
tion, as a friend that is closer than a brother; as a brother in
Christ. [Pray for me earnestly.] Provoke me to love and to
good works. . . . Join with me in the work of God; and let
us go on hand in hand."[18] That all people are of one family
and that each individual person is important to God has,
of course, always been at the heart of the gospel of Jesus
Christ. But it was Methodist preachers who took that truth
to the fields and mines, to people in all stations of life so
that they could hear it proclaimed with great feeling and
emotion, great concern and love. The intensity of the
Methodist movement unlocked energy to demonstrate this
love in action. And, if each individual is important, then
nonessentials must not be allowed to be a hindrance to the
gospel.

Methodism implies diversity. Through our diversity we
proclaim the gospel of God's love for all people. If we lose

our distinctive virtue of open-minded biblical faith with its resulting diversity, we cannot answer God's call to tell the gospel story in a way people embedded in modern cultures can understand. But the story we tell must truly be the gospel! The crisis of United Methodism is that Methodists on both ends of the liberal-conservative continuum have lost their focus on the *biblical* message. Some United Methodists have allowed themselves to be distracted by the traditional trappings and cultural overlays of religion that are not essential to the heart of the gospel. Some other United Methodists have so accommodated to the secularism of modern culture that they have lost sight of the essentials of the biblical faith, including the transcendence of God as the ground of moral absolutes. Today this crisis is most visible in our debate over homosexuality. This issue is important in itself, but it is also a symptom of the inability or unwillingness of people called Methodists to come to grips with the underlying problem of allowing the Holy Spirit to pour the eternal gospel of Jesus Christ into the new wineskins of our modern culture.

> The distinctive character of Methodism is imperiled by the loss of even a small minority of congregations at either end of the spectrum.

After their study of UMC leaders, Daniel Olson and William McKinney consider the question of schism. "Does the great internal diversity of United Methodism mean that it is likely to split apart? While some congregations and members may leave the denomination, we think schism is unlikely."[19] I agree with their basic argument that, since conflict has been institutionalized within the UMC, the UMC as an organization is not in jeopardy. For example, my survey shows that almost two-thirds of the delegates agree that "Caucus groups play a legitimate role in shaping General Conference decisions." By giving them voice, such groups tend to hold a diversity of members in the UMC. However, we must not underestimate the impact on *Methodism*, that is, the distinctive character of the UMC, of losing even a small minority of congregations at either end of the liberal-conservative spectrum. If we can't lead our own congregations to the culturally aware biblical faith that can sustain our unity, how can we lead people and societies to such a faith? Our challenge is to raise the consciousness of conservative United Methodists of the role of culture in mediating God's revelation, and then to accept *their* challenge to recover the Wesleyan zeal for the essentials of the Christian faith. (I will discuss this point in more detail in chapter 3).

As discussed above, despite the newspaper headline, the delegates were actually about evenly split in their reaction to the fifteen bishops. Many applauded them for opening up the subject—at least they forced us to see our differences. Other leaders at all levels of the church should follow suit. What the bishops did *not* do however was to place the discussion in the context of our Methodist heritage, which provides considerable resources for resolving our differences. Claiming our heritage is the topic of chapter 2.

CHAPTER TWO
Claiming Our Heritage

When the early circuit riders and missionaries struggled to the foot of the Rockies, where Native Americans were already at home, did they ever imagine the future? Did they conceive of a time when nearly 1,000 delegates plus their reserves, 125 bishops, and 2,000 staff and visitors would gather in Denver to celebrate and map the future of a worldwide, vibrant United Methodist Church?

But on Day One of the 1996 United Methodist General Conference it happened, beneath the familiar cross and flame symbol and the theme: "In Essentials Unity, In Non-Essentials Liberty, In All Things Charity."

The opening procession for the Communion service began with the cross lifted high, followed by the bishops from Africa, Asia, Europe, and the United States. Bishop Sharon Brown Christopher and Bishop Woodie W. White served as liturgist and celebrant respectively.

In his sermon, Bishop Roy I. Sano challenged delegates to embrace a future which appreciates the distinctive contributions of women, people of color, and those marginalized. "The past will be surpassed, but not supplanted," he said. "New surprises and new possibilities await us. Let us keep open to new possibilities and respectful of our past."[1]

A vibrant church united on the essentials of the faith! Was this account simply the hype that might be expected from an official publication? Was it the wishful thinking of a loyal United Methodist? I didn't think so. Though there was much said in the press about controversy before, during, and after the General Conference, I suspected that the controversial issues were not at the forefront of most delegates' thoughts most of the time. My observations of the 1996 General Conference encouraged me to expect that it was more about unity than about division; more about community than about controversy, and for most delegates, more about spirituality than about bureaucracy. Still the social scientist in me wanted solid data to support these impressions. My survey of delegates provided those data. Every four years elected delegates from around the world meet as the General Conference to celebrate, worship, dialogue, deliberate, and legislate for The United Methodist Church. These delegates play a vital role in the life of the church. According to the *Discipline*, "No person, no paper, no organization, has the authority to speak officially for The United Methodist Church, this right having been reserved exclusively to the General Conference under the Constitution."[2] Most United Methodists likely spend little time thinking about the General Conference. Some of those who do think about it may consider it a tool of bureaucracy, simply rubber stamping what church leaders want and little concerned with the spiritual life of the church. A thoughtful book by Paul A. Mickey and Robert L. Wilson, *What New Creation?* may inadvertently have contributed to this impression. Critiquing the process of restructuring the UMC (and other major denominations), the book raised the question

> Many delegates' positions on issues were affected by what they learned at the General Conference.

> whether a complex proposal worked out by a special committee over a period of time, such as a plan for reorganization of the denomination's national bureaucracy, can be effectively altered by the legislative body. The national

assembly has the power to do this; however, major changes are rarely made. The delegates meet for only a short time, generally less than two weeks. They have a large number of complicated matters with which to deal.[3]

Speaking specifically of the UMC General Conference's approval of restructure, they say: "While there was surprise at the ease with which the new structure was adopted, the battle had in fact been won before the delegates left home."[4] In important ways delegates' responses to my questions paint a different picture of the working of General Conference from that of Mickey and Wilson. Many delegates were impressed with the way in which they had conscientiously worked through mountains of petitions and numerous proposals. Forty-one percent said that something they "learned or experienced at the General Conference" caused them to change positions on an issue—or to make up their mind on an issue about which they were undecided. Twenty-eight percent of those who changed their minds did so on the ministry study. Twenty-four percent changed their mind on some homosexual issue. (Of these, 65 percent said they became more accepting of homosexual persons.) Other issues mentioned were ecumenicity (including the Consultation on Church Union), Baptism, restructure, and the Korean Missionary Conference. And, as we will see, most delegates appreciated the spiritual dimension of the General Conference.

Focusing on the 1996 General Conference and its delegates, this chapter asks whether central themes of our Methodist heritage still have power to bind us together. Central themes rooted in our Wesleyan heritage include biblical religion that is experienced, openness to theological and social diversity, geographical and social outreach, connectionalism, and social action as an expression of faith.

Biblical Religion That Is Experienced

Methodism is experienced religion. Wesley, himself, found his "heart strangely warmed" as he participated in a Bible study group. For Wesley the Bible was the basis for a living faith. He saw as one of the distinctive elements of his message the conviction that believers can "go on to perfection" by which he meant "constant communion with God the Father and the Son fills their hearts with humble love."[5] For one thing that means a life sustained by prayer. Wesley's spiritual religion was alive and well at the conference. The theme that emerged most clearly from the delegate data was that of a deeply spiritual faith. Roughly 23 percent of delegates volunteered this emphasis on spirituality, discernment, prayer time together, worship, preaching, or communion as the high point of the conference.[6] Asked about events and actions strengthening "the sense of community of United Methodists," 43 percent of the delegates listed this theme. Predictably, conservative delegates described such spiritual high points.[7] One conservative delegate saw the high point of the conference in "the mantle of prayer that encompassed all persons, every event, all objections and agreements." Another described "a feeling of the presence of the Holy Spirit, which enabled the passage of legislation which had been pending for several quadrennia." Liberals were equally moved by the spiritual aspects of the conference. One liberal delegate observed: "This conference was more intentionally and experientially spiritually centered than the three previous conferences that I have been a delegate." Another applauded "the experience of prayer with one another each day, all day." Still another liberal praised "the discernment times," which "were the thread which ran through the General Conference procedures."

> Prayer and worship are powerful resources for the unity our mission requires.

Many delegates referred specifically to the way in which the bishops had "wrapped the conference in prayer." The following selection from the Episcopal address describes the role of prayer the bishops envisioned.

> The delegates to this General Conference were invited to prayer, using a common daily guide for the forty days preceding our gathering. It made us one before we saw each other. Your Bishops now offer a specific sign of continuing prayer. Members of the Council of Bishops will be in prayer around the clock for the duration of this General Conference. We have designated teams of prayer partners who will intercede for all of us, asking the Holy Spirit to intrude into all we dream and propose, all we say and decide. We will identify the intercessors each day and the place where they are in prayer. Others may join them there, or in one of the other chapels, or a place of your own choosing. We invite all to join us in making this entire General Conference a season of prayer.
>
> In the same spirit, we ask that each time you gather in a legislative committee, in a caucus meeting, in plenary, you begin with five minutes of reflecting with another person—perhaps someone you do not know well—speaking about these two questions: 1) What is my most earnest hope for the next few hours of this General Conference? 2) What do I believe is God's most fervent hope for these next few hours? Then we ask you to pray with that conversation partner beseeching God to bring the two hopes into one. We go to our discipline of intercessory prayer with confidence God will break in with energy, wisdom and joy.[8]

We will see in chapter 3 that sharp theological differences lie at the root of different views toward homosexuality. Nevertheless, the continuing Methodist heritage of prayer and worship, which occasion God's breaking into our lives "with energy, wisdom, and joy," is a powerful resource for the unity our mission requires.

The Appreciation of Theological and Social Diversity

In 1788 Wesley said to a congregation in Glasgow:

The Methodists alone do not insist on your holding this or that opinion; but they think and let think. Neither do they impose any particular mode of worship; but you may continue to worship in your former manner, be it what it may. Now, I do not know any other religious society, either ancient or modern, wherein such liberty of conscience is now allowed, or has been allowed, since the age of the Apostles. Here is our glorying; and a glorying peculiar to us. What Society shares it with us? [9]

In a later sermon, "Catholic Spirit," Wesley elaborates: "My sentiment is, that I ought not to forbid water, wherin persons may be baptized; and that I ought to eat bread and drink wine, as a memorial of my dying Master: However, if you are not convinced of this, act according to the light you have."[10] Wesley appealed to all those who love God with heart, mind, and soul, and love as themselves "all mankind without exception," showing that love by doing good to "neighbours or strangers, friends or enemies, good or bad," or even if sincerely desirous of this state—then your heart is as my heart, then "give me thine hand." Love me as a friend, pray for me, "provoke me to love and to good works," "join with me in the work of God; and let us go on hand in hand."[11]

Nine percent of the delegates referred to tolerance, spirit of unity, openness, charity amidst debate, or diversity as the high point of the conference.[12] This was another theme highlighted by conservatives and liberals alike:

> Most delegates saw evidence of tolerance at the conference.

The spirit of Christ-centered focus on how to effect positive changes where we can and be unified in that (Conservative).

The spirit of the delegates as relating to one another and the Holy Spirit (Liberal).

Charity shown during fervent and emotional debates (Conservative).

The overall mood of loving acceptance which transcended intense disagreements (Moderate).

The civility and feeling of caring for each other—even when we disagreed (Liberal).

Most delegates saw evidence of tolerance at the conference. For example, despite sharp differences on the most controversial issues, 85 percent agreed that "The decision process within my legislative committee was fair and balanced." Without the quality of tolerance, diversity can hardly persist. The description of the opening communion service with which I began this chapter shows our commitment to diversity. The liturgist was a woman bishop, the celebrant was an African American bishop. The preacher, President of the Council of Bishops and himself an Asian American, spoke of "the distinctive contributions of women, people of color, and those marginalized." And soon after, the Episcopal Address was given by a woman bishop. Perhaps more than any other major religious body in the United States, The United Methodist Church affirms diversity. The diversity of the church goes beyond its world scope to include diversity of various religious, social, and political categories. A strong majority affirmed diversity. For example, 78 percent disagreed with the statement, "The UMC has become too diverse." And 77 percent agreed that "It is important that the General Conference decisions reflect the diversity within our denomination." Once more, these sentiments pervade the church. At least 70 percent of the delegates in each jurisdiction agreed with these statements. A recent survey of UMC leaders bolsters my study's findings on the support for diversity within the UMC. In their study of 359 "staff of national-level agencies, staff of state or regional level agencies, and board members of national-level policy-making boards" Daniel Olson and William McKinney found a broad range of diversity on matters related to evangelism, social activism, and other aspects of church life. Along with the diversity, they found a high degree of tolerance for diversity. They suggest that "given the high value that is placed on diversity and tolerance for diversity, one would . . . expect there to be greater respect and mutual recognition of these differences" than in the more conservative denominations.[13]

Geographical and Social Outreach

The second theme—global outreach, as well as social diversity discussed later—are related to Wesley's conviction that God calls *all* to salvation; and to Wesley's determination to cut across every boundary, geographical and social, to offer God's call, and to reach out to all the world in acts of human kindness. At the conference the notion that "the world is our parish" was evident in the opening procession with bishops from four continents. The Council of Bishops presented a progress report on their Study of the Global Nature of the Church. The following short excerpt from the bishops' global vision shows how our global outreach stems from our biblical faith:

A new spirituality for a global Church in a globalizing world is likely to entail the following considerations:

i.   Deepen and broaden the understanding of God the Spirit in such a way that no level or dimension of reality is outside His sphere.

ii. Overcome the conflict between matter and spirit in the tradition of Christian spirituality towards a synthesis that is more fruitful for Christian life in today's world.

iii. Facilitate a creative relationship between "the practice of the Presence of God" and the variety of cultures and their encounter, which today are the matrix for living the Christian faith.

iv. Undergird and nourish a global Church with a vital spirituality that will sustain it as it becomes more globally inclusive in its membership and seeks to respond more missionally to the needs of a global age.

Of course, the Spirit is free to blow where it wills, and the renewal of spirituality is not at the beck and call of human initiative. But globalizing The United Methodist Church might just be the occasion and motive for "the people called Methodist" to gather together in a "global room" and wait in anticipation for a new Pentecost that will once again make peoples "hear God's deeds of power" in their "own native language" (Acts 2:7-11).[14]

Adding to those who listed some aspect of the global nature of the church those who listed the arrival and speech of Bishop Arthur Kulah, which symbolized the global church, we find 28 percent of the delegates choosing the global emphasis as the high point of the conference. When asked about what strengthened the sense of community, 20 percent of the delegates listed the global character of the conference and of the church. One delegate commented: "Seeing the depth and breadth of our church. It is one thing to know we are a worldwide church. It is another thing to experience it." According to another delegate, "Bishop Kulah's entry and his welcoming speech gave us a greater sense of unity and that we truly are a global church." Still another delegate believed that "The worship experiences helped us to be a world-wide group."

One delegate, who considered herself conservative in religion but liberal on social issues, saw the global church theme in Hillary Rodham Clinton's address: "Mrs. Clinton's appearance [was the high point]—especially her reference to her time spent in UM Sunday School. 'Jesus loves the little children—all the children of the world.'"

Though it complicates our attempts to resolve the crisis over homosexuality in the United States (see chapter 3), the global character of the UMC is, on balance, a force for unity. Not only is the world our parish, our global church draws from throughout the world the physical, intellectual, and spiritual resources required for our mission.

The Connection

Another theme of Methodism is the connection. The connection provides a structure for action and spiritual mission, a mechanism for maintaining diversity and a context for tolerance. For many delegates the high point of the conference was the arrival of Bishop Kulah from war-torn Liberia. It was a dramatic moment, and a strong confirmation of the connection:

"Is there any hope for us?" Even as I raise this question they [the Methodists of Liberia] are very thankful to you, and I am to you, for the prayers you have offered on our behalf, for the support you have given to us for the past few months, the years. I want to thank you for everything you have done to keep us moving as a people. Without your prayers, without your support, without your cooperation, our annual conference wouldn't have been where it is today. . . . For with your prayers and your support, the church in Liberia shall rise again. Thank you very much.[15]

The Episcopal address also celebrated the connection.

So much of life waits for the healing touch of the Gospel. Sometimes it is mediated through human institutions, in systems and structures by which life is ordered. The General Conference is responsible for providing order and visible framework for United Methodism. That organization makes possible our carrying the Gospel's healing touch.

We are a people who value structure. We understand the strength of being connected with each other in orderly fashion that allows the flow of resources and the linking of gifts. Any decisions that weaken the coherence of that connection threaten the urgency of solidarity in witness and practice in a fractured world. So much in life suffers from discontinuity and disconnection. Our connection—manifested in structural coherence that is recognizable from place to place—is a sign of healthy wholeness. It is the means by which we are in ministry together where no one part of us can be effective alone.[16]

The delegates spent much of their time in legislative committees. My one specific question about the connection was related to the process of forming official positions on public issues. More than three-quarters of the delegates agreed that "One strength of the UMC system is that its positions on public issues are set by the General Conference where delegates have the opportunity to learn about issues and discuss them fully." At least 70 percent of delegates in each jurisdiction agreed.

Much of this conference dealt with the need to restructure the connection. Some delegates listed the granting of new flexibility in structure as the high point of the conference. More delegates saw restructuring as "strengthening the sense of community of United Methodists." But mainly the delegates discussed restructure in response to question 2, "What action taken by the 1996 General Conference do you think has the most significance for the United Methodist Church?"

Forty-six percent of the delegates listed some structural change as first or second choice for most significant action at the conference. It seems clear, however, that they want to strengthen the connection rather than weaken it. Here are some typical comments:

"[The new structure process is a] rejection of attempts to make us more congregational."

"It will be [the most significant action] if as a church we begin to function in ways that help us realize that being connected is a blessing and not a curse."

"Our United Methodist system has become top-heavy, too large, and cumbersome. While we achieve great things through our connection and it must be kept strong, my prayer is that a different system will allow us to do better at making disciples."

"[The Connectional Process Team] seems to be an opening to listen to each other and become a team in 'churching' in order to revitalize connectional nature of UMC."

"This frees up annual conferences and local churches for mission while still retaining the connectional relationship of United Methodism."

"Churches have found our presently mandated organizational format cumbersome and limiting for years. Flexibility opens avenues of creativity. Creativity allows for new movements of God's spirit."

I will have more to say about the connectional system in chapter 6, "Honoring Our Agreements." Meanwhile it is important to understand that connection is not only a structure for sustaining faith but also for facilitating action.

Social Action as an Expression of Biblical Faith

Methodists are deeply spiritual in their faith; Methodist faith is also linked with social action. Wesley asked "Whether we can be happy at all hereafter, unless we have, according to our power, 'fed the hungry, clothed the naked, visited those that are sick, and in prison,' and made all these actions subservient to a higher purpose, even the saving of souls from death?"[17] Wesley's "Holy Club" joined social action with faith, visiting those in prison and raising small sums to set some of them free. They also gave money to help artisans. Later, much of Wesley's preaching displayed a biblically based concern for the social structures in which people live.[18] For example, Wesley opposed not just liquor but the liquor trade. He attacked the institution of slavery. He understood that the employment of child labor was part of an unchristian system. No wonder many American Methodists were later attracted to the Social Gospel movement. A principal leader of that movement, Walter Rauschenbusch, taught that Jesus was fully aware of the importance of the social context in which people develop and act as responsible individuals. "It is not enough to christianize individuals; we must christianize societies, organizations, nations, for they too have a life of their own which may be made better or worse. Christ addressed Capernaum and Bethsaida as responsible personalities. He lamented over Jerusalem as a whole."[19] One way the theme of social action came through clearly in my survey was in delegates' responses to the address of Hillary Rodham Clinton. Almost a fourth of the delegates (24 percent) listed that address as either first or second as the high point of the Conference.

Mrs. Clinton stressed the link between personal faith and action on behalf of others.

> The church was a critical part of my growing up. And in preparing for this event, I almost couldn't even list all the ways it influenced me, and helped me develop as a person, not only on my own faith journey, but with a sense of obligation to others.[20]

A middle-aged delegate who described himself as conservative in religious matters but liberal on social and political matters said the high point of the conference was: "Hillary Clinton's speech and affirmation of Methodism's balance of personal faith and social action." Another delegate who considers himself a liberal applauded "Hillary Clinton's statement of the theological grounding for social justice."

An elderly delegate who considers herself a conservative said: "Mrs. Clinton's address [was the high point] because at the end she received a standing ovation from liberals and conservatives alike." Two questions specifically addressed the theme of social action. Eighty percent of the delegates agreed that "Avoiding positions on public issues is a betrayal of our Wesleyan heritage." Eighty-three percent agreed that "The UMC should lead the way in finding solutions to public issues." This strong endorsement of social action cuts through geographic jurisdiction. More than three-quarters of delegates in each jurisdiction agreed with these statements.

Signs of Unity

Most delegates do see signs of church unity. The survey data included responses to four direct questions about unity. Seventy-two percent of the delegates agreed that "The plenary sessions allowed the

> Most delegates see signs of church unity.

development of unity." Seventy-nine percent agreed that "On the whole, the General Conference tended to bring delegates together rather than to divide them." When delegates focus on their personal experience at the conference rather than general impressions, even more of them see signs of unity. Only 16 percent agreed with the statements "My personal sense of community within the UMC was lessened by attending the 1996 General Conference"; and "Deliberations in my legislative committee tended to be divisive."

Because there are significant regional variations in delegates' views on some contested issues, it is important to note here that most delegates in each geographical jurisdiction see signs of unity. Though the percent of delegates from the Southeastern Jurisdiction seeing signs of unity as measured by these four questions is a bit lower than in other jurisdictions, the lowest percentage is 64. Delegates' experiences related to these common themes of Methodism are a firm foundation for the unity required as we lead people and societies to a culturally aware biblical faith.

Undoubtedly, as Bishop Sano's sermon suggested, "New surprises and new possibilities await us." Yet responses to my survey reveal a vibrant United Methodist Church in which most delegates claim their common heritage and few are preoccupied with the homosexuality issue.

Still the crisis over homosexuality persists. For many devout and loyal United Methodists this issue has become a test of one's belief in the authority of the Bible. As stated earlier, the crisis over homosexuality will not be fully resolved until all are assured that the resolution upholds the authority of the Bible and opens the church to the power of the God of the Bible. Talking about the Bible is the topic of chapter 3.

Chapter Three
Talking About the Bible

The question has arisen whether we foresee the time we will welcome people of other racial groups. This question cannot be answered today, but I do want to indicate additional questions raised by this one: (1) What does the New Testament say about Christian faith expressed in race relationships? (2) How would Jesus answer the matter of racial attitudes and race relationships? Is the church in the first place "Christ's church," or do we consider it as "our church primarily"? What are some of the conclusions to be drawn in each answer? As your pastor, I present these questions to which I hope you will give serious thought, study, and prayer.

This statement was made by a pastor in a racially changing neighborhood who addressed a board reluctant to face the issue of welcoming African Americans to their church. It was several months before this church decided to welcome African Americans, but the pastor had placed the issue in a context that allowed members to move in that direction. The deliberations became a conversation about the Bible rather than an emotional argument about opinions.

My research on church leaders facing controversial issues shows that they lead best when they remind people what the church is, what people believe *as members of the church*. The above example comes from my study of fifty-eight Indianapolis congregations in 1973. I first polled members of each congregation about how their congregation should seek justice for the poor and for racial minorities. Then I examined the budgets, programs, building use, and official statements and policies of each congregation to see how the congregation was actually involved in the community. There was a clear conclusion: The actual community activism of most congregations *exceeded* the member support expressed in the poll. Why? Leaders of these congregations had framed policies on social action to reflect their biblically based understanding of the church as the servant of a just and compassionate God. Then these leaders used the Bible as a basis for persuading members to accept these policies. The account that began this chapter is a good example. By turning discussions on issues from arguments about opinions to conversations about the Bible, these leaders were able to secure members' support for the congregation's community ministry.

Why is it so important that discussions about controversial issues become conversations about the Bible? The Bible reminds us who we are, collectively as Christ's church and individually as members of the church. Much of this reminding comes in the context of controversies in the earliest churches. The Bible helps us to be more objective about issues by focusing on God and God's purposes rather than on ourselves and our purposes. This focus helps to clarify the nature of church unity.

> The church is the servant of a just and compassionate God.

Though the Bible reveals some timeless absolutes, it also shows that the appropriate application of these truths to specific situations is often not easy to discern. And the Bible connects us with the living God for understanding and for power.

The Early Church as an Example

As an extended example of how talking together about the Bible helps us to resolve controversial issues, let's consider 1 Corinthians. Writing to the Christians at Corinth, the apostle Paul first clarifies the ownership of the church. In the very first sentence he addresses "the congregation of God's people at Corinth, dedicated to him in Christ Jesus, claimed by him as his own, along with all men everywhere who invoke the name of our Lord Jesus Christ—their Lord as well as ours" (1:2 NEB). The church is God's church. We belong to God. "You belong to Christ, and Christ to God" (3:23 NEB). We are instruments of God's purpose. "Now you are Christ's body, and each of you a limb or organ of it" (12:27 NEB). The church is the body of Christ and we are individually members of it. An important part of that purpose is winning others for Christ: "I am a free man and own no master; but I have made myself every man's servant, to win over as many as possible" (9:19 NEB). "Work for the Lord always, work without limit, since you know that in the Lord your labour cannot be lost" (15:58 NEB). William M. Easum put it well: "Life in Christ comes to us on the way to someone else, congregations should focus outward instead of inward, congregations exist for those who are not part of them, life is meant to be given away not kept."[1] Our unity comes from all being God's people, not from agreement on styles of ministry or on signs of faith. Some might prefer Paul's ministry, others Apollos's. Those who were circumcised should be content, but those who have not been circumcised did not need to be. Some could eat meat dedicated to idols, others could decide not to. Paul allowed individual judgment on some issues. But all would be done in a framework of faith. "If food be the downfall of my brother, I will never eat meat any more, for I will not be the cause of my brother's downfall" (8:13 NEB). Just as some Methodists who recognized that some people can use beverage alcohol responsibly nonetheless pledged to abstain as a witness to the fact that one can live a full life without alcohol.

We are held to high standards of morality, precisely because we do belong to Christ. On the issue of prostitutes: "Do you not know that your bodies are limbs and organs of Christ? Shall I then take from Christ his bodily parts and make them over to a harlot? Never!" (6:15-16 NEB). On shunning fornication: "Do you not know that your body is a shrine of the indwelling Holy Spirit, and the Spirit is God's gift to you?" (6:19-20 NEB). Clearly boasting, greed, idolatry, reviling, drunkenness, joining with prostitutes, committing adultery, thievery, "the union of a man with his father's wife" (5:1 NEB), and "homosexual perversion" (6:9 NEB) are not acceptable. The only sure guide is love. "The best way of all" is love (12:31 NEB). "Let all you do be done in love" (16:13 NEB). "Put love first" (14:1 NEB). And what is love?

> Moral issues are complex and we have to work on understanding them.

> Love is patient; love is kind and envies no one. Love is never boastful, nor conceited, nor rude; never selfish, not quick to take offence. Love keeps no score of wrongs; does not gloat over other men's sins, but delights in the truth. There is nothing love cannot face; there is no limit to its faith, its hope, and its endurance. (13:4-7 NEB)

Yet moral issues are complex and we have to work on understanding them. On some issues (divorce, for example) Paul felt confident he was representing the Lord; on others he ventured his own judgment ("On the question of celibacy, I have no instructions from the Lord" [7:25 NEB]). On the matter of staying married to a heathen spouse, "I say this, as my own word, not as the Lord's" (7:12 NEB). Some might best marry, others not. The fact is that we often cannot be certain what is the right thing to do. In hindsight we may often see that we have made the wrong decision. My favorite professor in seminary, H. Richard Niebuhr, began a lecture on Christian ethics with the sentence: "Christian ethics comes under the head of repentance."

Imagined Correspondence with the Apostle Paul

An imagined exchange from a present day church to the apostle Paul will help us think about how he might approach some of the troublesome issues we face:

Dear Apostle Paul:

The grace and peace of the God and Father of our Lord Jesus Christ be with you. This letter seeks your advice on several matters that have arisen in our church. First, our college students are telling us that most students on campus engage in sexual relationships with little thought to longtime commitments and that many students treat the sex act like a handshake—no need to have met the person before, no need to expect to see that person again. Moreover, even some of our finest young people who strongly believe in marriage, once finding the person they intend to marry are setting up housekeeping weeks or even months before actually being married. And some of our widowed seniors, discovering that remarrying creates financial problems with Social Security payments and health care, are quietly living together as though married. Some are even asking their minister to bless such unions. What is your advice?

Sincerely,
Anywhere United Methodist Church

I can readily imagine that the Apostle's answer to the first question would condemn casual, promiscuous use of sex in no uncertain terms. But I wonder whether Paul's treatment of the other two questions might be more pastoral—"maybe it would be better to do this," but "depending on the circumstance" maybe that could be acceptable

> Paul's letters often show him in a pastoral mode.

so long as these relationships really do build up one another in love. Paul was in that pastoral mode, for example, when he discussed the circumstances the unmarried and widowed should consider before deciding for themselves whether to marry (1 Corinthians 7). Listen in with me to Paul's imagined reply:

From Paul, apostle of Jesus Christ at God's call and by God's will, to the congregation of God's people in Anywhere, USA, who are claimed by God as his own, along with people everywhere who invoke the name of our Lord Jesus Christ—their Lord as well as ours.

On the matters you wrote about. First, consider the promiscuous sexual relationships of your youths on college campuses. Have you not taught them that their bodies are limbs and organs of Christ? Do they know that their bodies are shrines of the indwelling Holy Spirit, and that the Spirit is God's gift to them? Of course we have the freedom to do anything. But is everything good for us? Does everything help the building of the community? Each must regard not just his or her own interests but the other person's as well. In these promiscuous relationships how likely is there to be the love that is marked by selflessness, kindness, and truthfulness; love that is patient and free of every conceit? To the contrary, such relationships provide occasion for abuse and exploitation. Sexual relations without this kind of love dishonor God and God's church.

Now the matter of those who intend to marry but live together before they are married. On this question I have no instructions from the Lord, but I give my judgment as one who by God's mercy is fit to be trusted. As you know our Lord has blessed and honored marriage. Doesn't it dishonor marriage for a couple to live together before marriage? If they have for each other the committed love God calls them to, then why not marry now? And if they have not this love, they should not be living together for they are living in sin.

Regarding your widows and widowers who do not marry because of social security and other financial considerations. Obviously it would be better if they would marry. What kind of signal are they sending to younger people about marriage? Are financial concerns really that important? Maybe the church could help them out if they really can't afford marriage. Still, "I have no wish to keep you on a tight rein" (7:35 NEB) on these last two matters. Perhaps each church and pastor will have to judge individual circumstances. The overriding concern is love. Do they truly exemplify the selfless love of marriage?

As a general rule, do not be quick to take offense. The most important thing is to build one another up in love. Sometimes that is hard—but remember God is the source of the power of transforming love. God is the source of power to serve, to remain in unity, to maintain high standards of morality. Even as I planted the seed of the gospel among you, and Apollos watered it; yet God made it grow (from 3:6-7). God is the source of power, but we can tap into that power; in fact, faith is "not a matter of talk, but of power" (4:20 NEB).

I wish you faith, hope, love and the joy of life in our Lord and Savior Jesus Christ, Paul.

Meeting the Living Christ

Obviously we cannot correspond with the apostle Paul. But the letters of Paul handed down by the church reveal a dynamic faith that views each situation in the light of God's love through Jesus Christ. Through these letters we meet the living Christ and receive power. G. Ernest Wright, in a marvelous book, *God Who Acts*, makes the point this way:

> Christian theology has tended to think of the Bible chiefly as "the Word of God," though in point of fact a more accurate title would be "the Acts of God." The Word is certainly present in the Scripture, but it is rarely, if ever, dissociated from the Act; instead it is the accompaniment of the Act. To speak of the Bible solely as the Word, as has been done so frequently, incurs the risk of obscuring this fact with the result that the Word becomes a substantive, dissociated from history and dealt with as an abstraction.[2]

The mid–nineteenth century hymn, "How Firm a Foundation," captures this nicely: The firm foundation is laid for our faith "in his excellent word!" And what does that excellent word say: "I am thy God and will still give thee aid."

What I have said above is very much in the Wesleyan tradition. Consider this extended excerpt from *The Book of Discipline*.

> United Methodists share with other Christians the conviction that Scripture is the primary source and criterion for Christian doctrine. Through Scripture the living Christ meets us in the experience of redeeming grace. We are convinced that Jesus Christ is the living Word of God in our midst whom we trust in life and death.
>
> As we open our minds and hearts to the Word of God through the words of human beings inspired by the Holy Spirit, faith is born and nourished, our understanding is deepened, and the possibilities for transforming the world become apparent to us. . . . Our standards affirm the Bible as the source of all that is "necessary" and "sufficient" unto salvation (Articles of Religion) and "is to be received through the Holy Spirit as the true rule and guide for faith and practice" (Confession of Faith).[3]

The phrase, "through the Scripture the living Christ meets us" is a strong assumption, yet one that has been validated for me and, I suspect, for many readers of this book, again and again. But if we stand on such solid common ground, why do we have the sharp differences discussed in chapter 1? The participants in the Theological Diversity Dialogues concluded that differences on homosexuality issues, as well as several fundamental theological differences—such as "the nature of Trinitarian faith, the meaning of incarnation, and our views of the saving work of Christ"—arise out of differing understandings of scriptural authority and revelation."[4] The delegate survey bolsters that conclusion. For example, one question asked whether God continues to reveal truth on the issues of homosexuality and abortion. Ninety-eight delegates believe that God's revelation does not continue. Most of these delegates (95 percent) do not believe that the UMC should ordain homosexuals. Three hundred sixty-three delegates say that God's revelation does continue. The majority of these delegates (54 percent) believe that the UMC should ordain homosexuals. On the question of permitting "homosexual marriages," 97 percent of the first group oppose such marriages, 60 percent of the second group oppose such marriages.

The Theological Diversity group encouraged further study and further dialogues on these issues. Such study and dialogue should pay more attention to the role of culture in mediating God's revelation to us. Taking culture into account clarifies, and may help to resolve, differences we have as we talk about the Bible.

Taking Culture into Account

Culture is "the integrated pattern of human knowledge, belief, and behavior that depends upon man's capacity for

> It is extremely difficult for people to comprehend anything that does not fit into the pattern of their culture.

learning and transmitting knowledge to succeeding generations."[5] People are so caught up in their culture that it is extremely difficult for them to comprehend anything that does not fit into its pattern. That is true of us, and it is true of the divinely inspired people who in the Bible reported God's revelations to them. Yet we have neglected to teach a cultural approach to the Bible even though it is implicit in our Wesleyan heritage. Witness these words from the *Discipline*:

> We properly read Scripture within the believing community, informed by the tradition of that community. We interpret individual texts in light of their place in the Bible as a whole.
> We are aided by scholarly inquiry and personal insight, under the guidance of the Holy Spirit. As we work with each text, we take into account what we have been able to learn about the original context and intention of that text. In this understanding we draw upon the careful historical, literary, and textual studies of recent years, which have enriched our understanding of the Bible.[6]

There are at least three ways in which a cultural understanding of the Bible would enlighten our discussions of the authority of the Bible. First, such an understanding helps us to see that the authority of the Bible is not threatened by our letting go of culture-bound practices that may have served earlier cultures in their relationship to God, but do not do so for us. In the New Testament we see early Christians struggling with many such practices. The practice of circumcision comes readily to mind. And the author of the book of Hebrews gave a stinging rebuke to those Jewish Christians who told Gentiles they could not be fully

> The authority of the Bible is not threatened by our letting go of culture-bound practices.

Christian unless they followed Jewish dietary restrictions: "It is good that our souls should gain their strength from the grace of God, and not from scruples about what we eat, which have never done any good to those who were governed by them" (Hebrews 13:8-9 NEB). Just as the early church learned that there were past religious practices that did not enhance their own relationship to God, we have to ask whether there are culturally bound formulations of the faith in the Bible that do not help us receive God's Holy Spirit in our lives and in our churches. Understanding how people are embedded in their cultures shows that literalistic or "proof-texting" approaches tear statements out of the integrated cultural fabric that gave them meaning. Given John Wesley's willingness to let Christians decide for themselves the "smaller matters," such as the form of baptism, or whether to baptize at all, Methodists should easily grasp the most important point here, that the cultural approach allows us to follow New Testament Christians in giving up some practices of the past without in any way undercutting our strong belief in the authority of the Bible.

The second contribution cultural awareness can make to our dialogues is to assure us that freeing universal truths from culture-bound formulations does not threaten the authority of the Bible. Though some past religious practices might be optional, there are fundamentals of our faith that are not optional. We may have genuine differences on what is fundamental, but much of what appears to be a difference on fundamentals may be a matter of language. Taking a cultural perspective may make our dialogues more fruitful. On the one hand, liberals must be encouraged to know and appreciate the biblical language of faith, both so that they can communicate with conservatives and potential Christians for whom the biblical language is salient and, even more important, as a safeguard that fundamental truths are not being lost in translation into the language of modern culture. On the other hand, conservatives may learn from the apostle Paul who became "all things to all men, that [he] might by all means save some." Following Paul's example surely entails making a determined effort to translate the fundamentals of the gospel into modes of thought understandable in modern cultures. We may never come to complete agreement on the essentials of Christian faith and practice, but we would make progress if liberals—as protection against losing sight of the transcendence of God—would learn the biblical language and conservatives—as a reminder that God is alive and at work in the world today—would join with liberals in attempts to communicate the fundamental truths in ways our culture can comprehend. This is not an easy task, but just undertaking the task together could contribute to our unity.

A third way cultural awareness can enlighten our dialogues is by showing why God cannot, at any given time, reveal all truth to any particular culture. It is not that God's fundamental truth changes. New capacities (or incapacities) to comprehend truth and new situations to apply it may emerge with each new generation or each new society. When in the Bible we meet the living Christ, we do so within our own culture. We cannot live in the Bible's culture.

> God's fundamental truth does not change.

Though we must understand that no culture can adequately receive God's revelation, we can only understand God's revelation within our culture. Specifically, if there is no knowledge or experience of a particular relationship and no language to describe it, we cannot communicate about it among ourselves—much less with God. The same is true, of course, of people within any culture, including the cultures that produced the Bible. That is why in my imagined letter I could not ask the apostle Paul about committed same-sex couples. I could not even imagine that he could comprehend a social phenomenon that has only recently emerged. His culture knew nothing of such couples as responsible members of the community. Failure to take this fact into account is a disservice to the Apostle, and it may cause us to misapply his ethical principles. For, though Paul's letters present an approach to Christian ethics that is applicable to the experience and language of modern cultures, we must take into account the limitations of Paul's experience and language as we use that approach.[7] The crucial truth we can learn from taking culture into account is that our differences are often matters of culture rather than faith. For example, making dialogues between conservatives and liberals culturally aware will help liberals understand that traditional formulations of the faith continually vitalize the faith of conservatives. At the same time, it will enable conservatives to see that liberals really do affirm the authority of the Bible. I have been referring to liberals and conservatives within the American culture. Thomas Edward Frank has highlighted how differences are compounded in a global context:

> An additional complicating factor in gender and sexuality issues is that an international denomination such as United Methodism has not only the conflicts of US society to contend with, but also the differing opinions and traditions of other cultures. Many societies are far less accepting of homosexuality than is the US. Women have yet to achieve leadership roles in most societies. This puts American Christians in a real dilemma. Should they advocate the gender and sexuality mores of a constantly changing US culture, thus becoming a revolutionary influence in traditional cultures? Or should they respect the cultures of other lands and allow churches there to exclude the very persons whose rights the American church has tried to protect?[8]

Though my book is addressed primarily to an American audience, my basic argument applies throughout the world. Cultural awareness will allow participants in the dialogues of the global church to face their real differences in the security of the knowledge that we all affirm the authority of the Bible. The need for this security was evident in the 1996 General Conference debate on removing the "incompatible with Christian teachings" phrase from the *Discipline*. Four of the seven delegates who spoke against removing the phrase were international delegates. Two of them emphasized that the proposed action would undermine the authority of the scriptures, the other two focused on the difficulty for people within their cultures to understand such an action. As we will see in chapter 5, these delegates had an important influence.

> We can face our differences secure in the knowledge that we all affirm the authority of the Bible.

As Methodists in the United States, Africa, Latin America or wherever, we cannot escape our cultures. But our biblical faith may enable us to transform our cultures even as we reflect them. The ethical principles of the New Testament can provide guidance for Christian living within every culture and may serve as leverage for transforming every culture.

Once we understand the impact of their culture on the way the people of the Bible received God's revelation, it is not so great a step to understanding that God's revelation today comes to us through our own culture, even though God may call us to transform our culture. Wesley, at least as preacher, approached the Bible expecting to receive additional revelation beyond that originally received by the Bible's authors. For example, in his famous sermon on "Catholic Spirit" he asks, "'Is thine heart right, as my heart is with thy heart?' But what is properly implied in the question? I do not mean, what did Jehu imply therein? But, what should a follower of Christ understand thereby, when he proposes it to any of his brethren?"[9]

With cultural awareness we can seek the Holy Spirit's

guidance in applying God's word to new events and experiences without weakening our strong belief in the authority of the Bible. The delegate survey shows that a cultural understanding of the Bible influences how we look at issues in our own culture. I categorized delegates according to the extent that they take into account the cultural context of the Bible in applying it to contemporary problems. I divided the delegates into biblical liberals ("The Bible was written by people inspired by God but contains some errors reflecting the limitations of the authors and the culture of their times"), biblical moderates ("The Bible is God's word, and it is authoritative for Christian faith and practice, but it is not a book of science or history"), biblical conservatives ("The Bible is God's word, and all it says is true, but not all of it is meant to be taken literally"), and biblical literalists ("The Bible is God's word, and it is meant to be taken literally word for word").

Less than 3 percent of the delegates hold biblical literalist views, 24 percent are conservative, 41 percent are moderate, and 32 percent are liberal. Since only sixteen delegates expressed literalist views, any generalizations about them are precarious. Still, we can note the possibility of associations between literalism and region (seven of the sixteen are from the Southeastern Jurisdiction, and none from the Western Jurisdiction) and between literalism and gender (eleven of the sixteen are men). Given our United Methodist heritage, the small percentage of biblical literalists is not surprising. Yet, surveys of the general U.S. population show more than a quarter of United Methodists with such views. The same polls show that more than half of Southern Baptists are biblical literalists. In 1996, 27 percent of United Methodists, compared to 58 percent of Southern Baptists, held literalist views. In contrast to the literalists, the biblical liberals are more prevalent in the West and less prevalent in the South, and they are more likely to be women. Forty-three percent of Western Jurisdiction delegates are biblical liberals, compared to 24 percent of Southeastern Jurisdiction delegates. Fifty-six percent of biblical liberals are women.

It is important to note that biblical liberals are not secularists. In an open question on the high point of the conference, 17 percent of biblical liberals listed spiritual and worship matters, slightly more than the other delegates (16 percent). Asked what most contributed to unity, 35 percent of biblical liberals, compared to 30 percent of other delegates listed prayer and discernment.

> Biblical liberals are not secularists.

Look at the difference taking culture into account makes for views on the homosexuality issues:

"Homosexuality is a sin"

Twenty-two percent of biblical liberals agree, compared to 48 percent of biblical moderates, 68 percent of biblical conservatives, and 13 of 16 biblical literalists.

"Homosexual marriages should be permitted within the UMC"

Fifty-one percent of biblical liberals agree, compared to 23 percent of biblical moderates, 16 percent of biblical conservatives, and one of the 16 biblical literalists.

"Homosexuals should be ordained within the UMC"

Fifty-nine percent of biblical liberals agree, compared to 29 percent of biblical moderates, 18 percent of biblical conservatives, and none of the 16 biblical literalists.

What are the implications, for liberals and for conservatives, of these findings that cultural awareness makes people more accepting of homosexual relationships? For one thing, the cultural awareness of liberals should alert them to the danger that in approving any same-sex relationships they may be misunderstood as affirming a physically and spiritually unhealthy lifestyle. They should take care that the relationships they approve meet the test of biblical morality, that is, that in mutual love and fidelity they build one another up in the kind of love that engenders responsibility for the community.

Conservatives for their part should take the liberals at their word of affirming the authority of the Bible, and accept the challenge to be open to the leading of the Holy Spirit in applying the eternal truths of the Bible within our culture. Consider this contribution to the plenary debate on "the incompatible with Christian teachings" phrase:

> I am a conservative Christian. . . . I have had many rela-tionships, dialogues over my years of ministry with gays and lesbians. I believe that we are at a point in our church life when we need to state exactly who we are and where we are so that we can move . . . into that arena of one-on-one dialogue. We need to continue the study; but more than study the conversation and relationship, trusting that God's spirit will give us wisdom to know how to interpret the scriptures; to know how to interpret the moving of the spirit for this day. Thank you very much.[10]

We can lead people and societies to a culturally aware biblical faith only if our own faith is strong. Who will remind us that as Methodists we are not only the people gathered around the Bible, but that we understand the Bible in light of the culture of those whom God inspired to write it? This is a task for bishops, the General Conference, the annual conferences, and the local pastors. Yet the laity may lead us! Thirty-six percent of the lay delegates, com-pared to 29 percent of clergy and 27 percent of superin-tendents, are liberal interpreters of the Bible.

The complexity of the subject of culture and revelation is illuminated in the following quotation from H. Richard Niebuhr's, *Christ and Culture*:

Given these two complex realities—Christ and culture—an infinite dialogue must develop in the Christian conscience and the Christian community. In his single-minded direction toward God, Christ leads men away from the temporality and pluralism of culture. In its concern for the conservation of the many values of the past, culture rejects the Christ who bids men rely on grace. Yet the Son of God is himself child of a religious culture, and sends his disciples to tend his lambs and sheep, who cannot be guarded without cultural work. The dialogue proceeds with denials and affirmations, reconstructions, compromises, and new denials. Neither individual nor church can come to a stopping-place in the endless search for an answer which will not provoke a new rejoinder.[11]

Our conversations about the issues that divide us must be conversations about the Bible because God's inspiration and power can be available in a special way when we talk about the Bible with persons of opposing views. For some Methodists we meet at the Bible to read its eternal words, for others to meet the eternal Word. There is an important difference. Still, as long as we keep the biblical dialogue going, we stand on common ground. Standing on that common ground, let us look at ways to open our minds (chapter 4) and enlarge our circles (chapter 5).

> God's inspiration is available in a special way when we talk about the Bible with persons of opposing views.

Chapter Four
Opening Our Minds

But some may say, I have mistaken the way myself, although I take upon me to teach it to others. It is probable many will think this, and it is very possible that I have. But I trust, whereinsoever I have mistaken, my mind is open to conviction. I sincerely desire to be better informed. I say to God and man, "What I know not, teach thou me!"[1]

This affirmation of open-mindedness is found in John Wesley's preface to a book of his sermons published in 1747. Usually when people quote Wesley's famous phrase, "think and let think," they stress the "let think"—the call for tolerance. That is important. But just as important is that Wesley wanted us, when faced with an issue, to use our minds rather than to respond ideologically. Methodism believes in reason. Nothing gets more in the way of resolutions of conflict than the insistence that one cannot reason about an issue. Wesley called us to think about information, to think about evidence, and to be open to new conclusions. He stood on firm biblical ground. Jesus said that the greatest commandment, the one that comes first is, "You shall love the Lord your God with all your heart, and with all your soul, and with all your mind" (Matthew 22:37). It is interesting to note that the Old Testament parallel statement does not include "mind." But Matthew, Mark, and Luke all report that Jesus included it. So this is one thought we do have from the Lord. Loving God with

> Methodism believes in reason.

our minds is essential to our mission of making disciples in contemporary society.

A Lost Evangelical Virtue

Mark Noll, an evangelical historian who teaches at Wheaton College, has stressed the importance of using our minds when we read the Bible. Noll bemoans the fact that American Fundamentalists of the late nineteenth and early twentieth centuries turned away from the evangelical tradition of taking into account the historical and cultural context of the Bible. The result has often been "an evangelical community unwilling to sift the wheat from the chaff in the wisdom of the world, unprepared to countenance the complexity of mixed motives in human action, and uninterested in focusing seriously on the natural forces that influence human behavior."[2] "With such an orientation, not only was the exploration of nature and ordinary human affairs suspect, but every possible barrier had been erected against the attempt to let the deep riches of Christian theology guide human understanding of the world."[3] Arguing that such features of fundamentalism as biblical literalism are innovations that are not essential and even get in the way of traditional evangelicalism, Noll is particularly disturbed that such an approach to the Bible does not "help the believer to find a biblical understanding of the world in which the believer lived."[4] Noll both exemplifies and foretells how evangelicals can stick to what he considers the heart of evangelicalism without taking a literalist view of the Bible.

Noll's view is compatible with our Wesleyan heritage, which draws strength from the spectrum of approaches to the Bible. As indicated earlier, few United Methodist leaders hold biblical literalist views. (Less than 3 percent of the 1996 General Conference delegates gave the biblical literalist response to my question about their views of the Bible.) Though about 27 percent of United Methodist members do hold such views, the percent has declined over the last ten years. My own conversations with Methodists confirm Bishop Michael Coyner's description of "The Methodist Middle":

> Those in the Methodist Middle value Scripture, but they are not biblical literalists, nor do they simply ignore Scripture when it fails to support their personal preferences. . . .
>
> Those in the Methodist Middle know that the really tough issues of our day, like homosexuality, are not resolved by name-calling, petitions or judicial processes. They know that medical science is divided on the question of whether people are homosexual by birth or by development (or by both). They know people who are homosexuals and who struggle to be faithful Christians, and they understand that the issue of homosexuality is not a simple one.
>
> They also know that the Scriptures are not silent on this issue, and they take that seriously, while seeking to learn from the best biblical scholarship to discover the context, meaning, and interpretation of those texts. They are aware that the traditions of the church have spoken against homosexual practice, and they respect those traditions. They also believe that God's Spirit continues to give the Church discernment on this issue, and they are willing to remain in the United Methodist Church to struggle with this difficult issue.[5]

Bishop Coyner may be right that 70 to 90 percent of all United Methodists fit this description. Yet I expect that many United Methodists in the pew absorb biblical literalism from the culture around them, especially in the South. That is why it is so important that we United Methodists reclaim our heritage of seeking a rigorous intellectual and culturally aware understanding of the Bible.

All the World's Knowledge

Loving God with our minds goes beyond biblical scholars and theologians, encompassing all of the world's knowledge. All truth is God's truth. At least for the Western world, this commandment may be one source of the development of views that public policy should be "born of the power of the better argument." "The idea that the best rational argument and not the identity of the speaker was supposed to carry the day was institutionalized as an available claim."[6] Our *Discipline* recognizes this in its discussion of human sexuality:

> We also recognize our limited understanding of this complex gift and encourage the medical, theological, and social science disciplines to combine in a determined effort to understand human sexuality more completely. We call the Church to take the leadership role in bringing together these disciplines to address this most complex issue.[7]

Noll emphasizes that all truth is God's truth by placing these intellectual disciplines in a religious light:

> For a Christian, the mind is important because God is important. Who, after all, made the world of nature, and then made possible the development of sciences through which we find out more about nature? Who formed the universe of human interactions, and so provided the raw material of politics, economics, sociology, and history? Who is the source of harmony, form, and narrative pattern, and so lies behind all artistic and literary possibilities? Who created the human mind in such a way that it could grasp the realities of nature, of human interactions, of beauty, and so made possible the theories on such matters by philosophers and psychologists? Who, moment by moment, sustains the natural world, the world of human interactions,

> Loving God with our minds goes beyond biblical scholarship, encompassing all of the world's knowledge.

and the harmonies of existence? Who, moment by moment, sustains the connections between what is in our minds and what is in the world beyond our minds? The answer in every case is the same. God did it, and God does it.[8]

The Social Principles of The United Methodist Church affirms both the value and the limitations of science: "We recognize science as a legitimate interpretation of God's natural world. We affirm the validity of the claims of science in describing the natural world, although we preclude science from making authoritative claims about theological issues."[9] From the social science perspective one of the most significant findings about sexual orientation is that gay men and lesbians are no more likely than heterosexuals to be emotionally unstable or to experience psychological problems. One team of researchers found that gay people in stable, intimate relationships were about as well adjusted as married people. "All in all, differences in adjustment seem more likely to reflect the life style than the sexual orientation."[10] These findings are especially interesting since it was not until 1973 that the American Psychiatric Association dropped homosexual orientation from its list of mental disorders.[11]

Forty-four percent of Americans think that homosexuality is at least partly something that one is born with.[12] In the light of Noll's argument, it is interesting to note that recent Gallup surveys show that those who consider themselves born again are much less likely (29 percent) than those who do not (65 percent) to believe that homosexuality is something that a person is born with.[13] A 1994 poll showed that 53 percent of United Methodists believe that sexual orientation is something an individual cannot change. The scientific evidence for this position is mounting. For example, whether due to genetic or other factors, there is a great deal of evidence that gay and lesbian sexual orientations run in families.[14] Evidence of genetic factors in sexual orientation includes several studies of twins showing that when one twin is gay, the other twin is more than twice as likely to be gay if the twins are identical twins rather than if they are fraternal twins. However, in view of the variability of individuals and the complexity of human behavior, it is unlikely that science will ever find a set of causal factors that fully explains sexual orientation.

As it happens some of the foremost scholars on sexuality are in my own university. To help me resolve in my own mind the issue of choice of sexual orientation, I interviewed five of these experts—a sociologist, a social psychologist, an anthropologist, a clinical psychologist, and a psychiatrist. These scholars think not just of heterosexual, bisexual, and homosexual orientations, but of a continuum that takes into account sexual attraction, sexual identification, and sexual behavior. They see a complex of causal factors that may include biological (for example, genetic predisposition and the influence of prenatal hormones), environmental (early experiences in childhood), and psychological (cognitive learning that attaches meaning to experience). These scholars did not completely agree about causes of homosexuality, yet there was a consensus that those persons high on the homosexuality scale could not change their sexual orientation. In fact, three of these experts strongly cautioned against the possibility of psychological damage resulting from pressing a person to change his or her sexual orientation. Here are a few sentences from Dr. Alan P. Bell's response to my question about whether persons can change their sexual orientation:

> I'd say it depends on the individual. There may be a very small number of gay males who, for a variety of reasons are able to enlarge their heterosexual potential, avoid homosexual contact, marry and be reasonably happy. That doesn't mean they've become heterosexual—they are still homosexual almost without exception. It is possible for

such people to function as heterosexuals. But I think that the number that can do it is very small. To make that kind of demand of homosexual men who are simply not in a position to even entertain the notion of becoming more heterosexual is to do them a grave, grave disservice. To suppose that most of them can ever be truly heterosexual and to make that demand or to encourage Herculean efforts in that direction only promotes discouragement, despair, despondency, and depression. Their personal integrity becomes lost in the bargain.

> Most homosexual persons cannot change their sexual orientation.

Dr. John Bancroft, the one of these five scholars who was most receptive to the idea that some persons could change their homosexual orientations, nonetheless warned against a failure to recognize that many homosexual relationships are valid or worthwhile objectives in their own right. In a 1983 paper he observed that "considerable moral harm has been done in society by condemning homosexual relationships, regardless of their nature, and by implication accepting heterosexual relationships whatever their nature."[15]

Based on my interviews and my reading on the subject of whether people can choose their sexual orientations, I reached three conclusions. First, it is likely that some people have changed their homosexual orientation. At the 1996 General Conference there were several emotional exchanges among delegates over the use of the term, "ex-gay." Some supporters of the rights of homosexual people were afraid the term implied that any homosexual person could become heterosexual. But others felt the term described their own experience or that of their friends. The debate ended when an article in *AFFIRM!*, the news sheet of Affirmation: United Methodists for Lesbian, Gay and Bisexual Concerns, suggested that we call people the names by which they want to be called. "The first essential of love is to respect the experiences and language of the other, to call them by their own names. In this case, love demands that we call ex-gays by the name they have chosen for themselves."[16] I believe that is the proper spirit. We should respect and rejoice with those who have changed their sexual orientation and those who helped them to change.

My second conclusion is that most homosexual persons cannot change their sexual orientation. We should accept them as they are. And all of us should encourage each other, whatever our orientations and relationships, to build one another up in that responsible love the apostle Paul describes in the thirteenth chapter of First Corinthians. Together as Christians we should teach and enable all persons to avoid promiscuity in sexual behavior. The counsel of a liberal woman General Conference delegate in her forties is instructive here:

> I wish we could acknowledge how much is not yet known about the biology and psychology of sexual orientation, and agree that Jesus' love commandment is our priority guide toward accepting each other in the church. Rather than focusing on sexual orientation or practice, I wish we could affirm fidelity in relationships, and focus our discontent on promiscuity, regardless of orientation.

My third conclusion is a theological one. The most important concern is not why people form particular relationships but the quality and impact of those relationships. In New Testament terms, are those relationships vehicles through which individuals receive and show the gifts of the Holy Spirit? Focusing on this question will move us toward resolution of the crisis over homosexuality in the UMC (see chapter 7).

God's Continuing Revelation

For Methodists, having open minds not only means reading the Bible mindfully and taking advantage of existing knowledge, it also means staying open to God's continuing revelation through increased knowledge and through events in our world, and using our minds to discern more direct urgings of God's Holy Spirit.

Because the question of God's continuing revelation is a contested issue among United Methodists, I want to address here a legitimate concern of those who believe that God's revelation is completed in the Bible. "If we believe in God's continuing revelation," they ask, "doesn't that open the doors to moral relativism, with each person having his or her own standard of the Christian life?" One might respond that, since Christian history is full of instances of ideologically driven interpretations of the scriptures, this real danger is not a new one. But, though partially true, this response does not treat the question with the seriousness it deserves. The truth is that some liberals in our society, possibly there are Methodists among them, may use the idea of the continuing revelation to avoid the demands of the authentic Christian life. Sociologist James Davison Hunter distinguishes between progressive and orthodox impulses in our society. Progressivism, according to Hunter, "is the tendency to resymbolize historic faiths according to the prevailing assumptions of contemporary life." Orthodoxy, by contrast, "is the commitment on the part of adherents to an external, definable, and transcendent authority."[17] It is an understatement to say that, from the perspective of historic Methodism, progressivism as Hunter defines it leaves much to be desired. Though Hunter recognizes that most Americans fall somewhere between these two extremes, he does not articulate the impulse of most United Methodist liberals—the tendency to resymbolize the historic faith so as to apply its transcendent truths to contemporary life. Perhaps I can describe poetically the difference between Hunter's progressive, who apparently

> United Methodist liberals and conservatives have more in common *theologically* than they sometimes think.

does not believe in the transcendent God, and my understanding of the United Methodist liberal, who does. David Head has said, "The two things about God that matter supremely are that He is a living God, and that He is very much like Jesus."[18] The progressive might agree, but the United Methodist liberal would want to add from the African American spiritual, "He's got the whole world in his hands." United Methodist liberals and United Methodist conservatives probably have more in common *theologically* than they sometimes think.

As discussed in chapter 3, I asked the 1996 delegates: "Do we know all we need to know to resolve the controversies over abortion and homosexuality within church and society, or might God yet reveal more truth on these matters?"

About 17 percent of delegates are confident that we have all we need to know on these issues. These delegates are primarily the biblical conservatives. The following are typical of their responses:

"I believe scriptures speak clearly to these issues. And I know God's word does not change" (a fifty-year-old woman).

"The Bible explains it all" (a fifty-seven-year-old man).

"The Bible is very clear on both issues if a person is willing to accept the scriptures" (a sixty-five-year-old man).

Just over two-thirds of the delegates believe that God may well reveal more that is relevant to these issues. Here are some of their responses:

"I think we are still learning about these issues. We need

to be open to new information and to God's leading" (forty-year-old woman).

"Hopefully, we are never closed to God's revelations. Only revelations from God can resolve such issues" (a fifty-two-year-old woman).

"No, we don't know all we need to know. We must continue to seek God's guidance" (a fifty-one-year-old woman).

"God continues to reveal God's truth through knowledge and reason" (a sixty-three-year-old man).

Some of those who expect God to reveal more on these issues expect that revelation to come through science.

"In regard to homosexuality, more scientific research will prove to be an avenue of God's continuing revelation" (a fifty-five-year-old man).

A sixty-five-year-old woman delegate who had earlier indicated that she would leave the UMC if its national position became too liberal on homosexuality, gave a particularly interesting response to this question:

"We are not yet what we shall become! If eventually, medical science proves new revelations, I'll listen."

> Delegates' beliefs about revelation strongly influence how they feel about homosexuality.

What delegates believe about continuing revelation strongly influences how they feel about homosexuality. For example, 91 percent of those who think God will not reveal more consider homosexuality a sin, but only 31 percent of those who think God will reveal more consider homosexuality a sin.

Challenging Others to Think

Allowing others to think—giving them permission to think, listening to their thoughts, indeed, challenging them to think and being challenged by them to think—is also important. Here is one motivation for Methodists' investment in educational institutions and their support of public education. The 1996 General Conference adopted a resolution reminding us that our "heritage is filled with vivid examples of Christlike concern for training the mind as well as nurturing the faith" and that "John Wesley was 'a unique and remarkable educator (who) gave to the whole Methodist movement throughout the world a permanent passion for education.' " The resolution called the Church to "join hands with educators in seeking more effective ways to prepare our children for a future in which they will both find personal fulfillment and make a significant contribution to the world." It also urged each local congregation to "develop a plan for concrete involvement in the educational activity of its community, seeking to improve the system, and becoming involved with students."[19]

> Fundamentalists have played a positive role in defending many essential Christian convictions.

The notion of dialogical thinking implied in Wesley's plea to "think and let think," was embodied in the process of the Committee to Study Homosexuality, in its report, in the study materials based on the report, and in the local congregations' use of the study materials. A seventy-year-old delegate who labeled himself a conservative on both religious and social matters appreciated this fact. He wrote in the survey:

> Encourage local congregations to read and discuss the Report/Study on Homosexuality submitted by GCOM at the 1992 General Conference. Obtain reactions from each Congregation who read and discussed the study.

A sixty-five-year-old woman delegate who considers herself liberal also underscored the importance of dialogue:

> We must first be willing to hear each others' positions as they exist, then study and talk together to discern where we need to move and bring about positive change.

Different perspectives may be necessary in seeking the truth. Noll applauds the fundamentalists for their defense of "many convictions essential to a traditional understanding of Christianity. At a time when naturalism threatened religion, when relativism assaulted social morality, when intellectual fashions were turning the Bible into a book of merely antiquarian interest, fundamentalists said what needed to be said about the supernatural character of religion, the objectivity of Christian morality, and the timeless validity of Scripture."[20] If the biblical conservatives in the UMC can help remind us of the transcendence of God, the objectivity of morality, and the timeless validity of Scripture, the biblical liberals can help the church to apply these truths in the world in which we live. Perhaps the tension of these conservative and liberal forces is healthy for the church. In the 1996 General Conference Laity Address, James Lane put it this way:

> Do we all look alike, think alike, understand and express God's love the same, hold the same, turn loose the same? Heavens no! Does that make any one of us any less, or any more, worthy of membership in this covenant community . . . ? Certainly not! We all need each other. Each one of us needs his or her own place to stand in this great congregation, but we also need each other.[21]

Our leaders need to challenge us to think. Loving God with our minds is essential to our unity and to our mission. One way to facilitate opening our minds is to enlarge our circles of concern and caring. Enlarging our circles is the topic of chapter 5.

CHAPTER FIVE
Enlarging Our Circles

I witnessed a dramatic moment in the Church and Society Legislative Committee during the 1996 General Conference. After a week of intense but mostly cordial discussions of homosexuality issues, it was clear that the committee was about evenly split on these issues. One specific issue was whether to leave in the *Discipline* the phrase, "Although we do not condone the practice of homosexuality and consider this practice incompatible with Christian teaching." Many members of the committee preferred to replace this phrase with an admission that United Methodists are not of one mind on the issue. The committee decided before taking a vote to have one more round of arguments. One of the key advocates for taking out the incompatibility phrase gave a reasoned, heartfelt and impassioned plea. Then a key advocate of leaving the phrase in the *Discipline* gave an equally reasoned, heartfelt, and impassioned plea. As this speaker, who had been sitting behind the first one, sat down, he squeezed his opponent's shoulder. In their anguished glances at each other, I sensed deep caring and respect for each other. Each had enlarged his circle of friendship and conversation to include the other. Neither could ever again see homosexuality as a simple issue.

The Bible's Mandate

The Bible again and again calls us to enlarge our circles of concern and caring. There is the emphasis on hospitality to strangers, rooted in faith that God cares for all. Most people know the story that Jonah was swallowed by a fish. Sometimes we forget why. It was because he did not want to include the people of Nineveh within his circle. Jesus pointedly called on his hearers to include the despised Samaritan in their caring. The early church found that enlarging their circles allowed God to loosen the grip of culture and bring about fundamental changes in their faith. Witness Peter's discovery that Gentiles could be acceptable to God (Acts 10 and 11).

A Sociological Truth

That changes in thought and action follow changes in networks of social interaction is a fundamental sociological truth. James S. Coleman highlights the importance of associations in which people of differing backgrounds come together for a common purpose creating cross-cutting social attachments. Such attachments create situations in which persons in one social group—let us say laborers or whites or the rich or evangelical Christians—associate with those in other social groups—let us say managers or blacks or the poor or liberal mainline Protestants. Circles of friendship that create cross pressures on individuals make them more aware of culture's grip on them. During a controversy cross-pressured persons can be more objective, more able to see all sides of an issue because, as Coleman argues, "One group of people to whom he [or she] feels close is on one side; others . . . equally close are on the other."[1]

People's ideas, values, and behaviors are influenced by their location within those networks of social interaction that sociologists call social structures. Essentially any patterned interaction

> Social change often comes about because people's circles of friendship change.

among a set of people is a social structure. Examples include the circles of friendship within neighborhoods, communities, occupational groups, and various organizations and associations (including churches). So when people differ in their opinions, we can ask whether they are located in different social networks that influence their opinions. These networks of interaction influence us at least in part because they facilitate carrying on serious conversations with some people and inhibit carrying on conversations with others. In other words, an individual's circles of friendship determine who he or she carries on conversations with; and those conversations tend to make particular ideas more (or less) believable. For example, it turns out that General Conference delegates from California are two and one-half times more likely to describe themselves as liberal in social and political matters than delegates from Georgia. We may assume that this difference is partly due to the fact that in a liberal state like California it is easier to carry on conversations that sustain liberal views than in a relatively conservative state like Georgia.

Sociologists assume that certain characteristics such as place of residence, age, gender, income, and education are associated with different circles of friendship. In other words, these characteristics influence who people talk to and what they talk about. These conversations in turn help shape and sustain individuals' values, beliefs, and behaviors. For example, persons in different educational categories may be more likely to discuss their political views with others of similar education. In fact, of those delegates with a bachelor's degree or less education, 52 percent consider themselves "conservative" in social and political matters, compared to 28 percent of those who have more than a bachelor's degree.

Social change often comes about because people's circles of friendship change; that is, they enlarge the circle of persons with whom they carry on serious conversations. Delegates from California may appreciate some conservative ideas better and delegates from Georgia may appreciate some liberal ideas better because they carry on conversations with each other at General Conference. The General Conference itself is a network of social interactions, which tends to broaden delegates' perspectives by facilitating conversations among people with diverse social backgrounds. A possible result of this broadening of perspective is a working consensus that is based more on the central values and common traditions of the church and less on regional or cultural variations. This is an important result. My thirty-five years of studying how churches deal with controversy has shown that effective leaders can dampen conflict within the church by reminding all parties of such values and traditions.

How Their Circles of Friendship Influence Delegates

A number of delegates see enlarged circles of relationships as contributing to the resolution of the issue of homosexuality. This truth is implicit in the frequent endorsement of "dialogue" by delegates throughout the conservative/liberal spectrum. For example, a seventy-one-year-old female moderate urges us to "have dialogue, listen to each other rather than debate and argue." Some delegates, however, are more explicit. Here are some of their responses:

"Gradual change is the best route, allowing persons to discuss, experience and grow together in their diversity (a fifty-year-old male conservative)."

"If we would concentrate more on loving our neighbors, rather than on who is right and who is wrong, then we would be closer to Christ's teachings. When more of us get to know marginalized people more personally, our prejudices are challenged. Everyone should be welcome in our churches" (a thirty-year-old female moderate).

"A common ground position is only possible if both sides would stop speaking for God. In time, as more and more UM's 'discover' homosexuality among their family members, close friends, and church members, this problem will go away" (a fifty-six-year-old male liberal).

"I don't think legislation will solve this issue. More attention to Jesus' lack of comment and the recognition by growing numbers of people that there are gays/lesbians in their own family will finally tip the balance" (a sixty-year-old male liberal).

"More dialogue among folks of diverse positions. Sharing personal stories, struggles is important and life changing" (a forty-eight-year-old delegate who describes herself as "very liberal").

"Know someone *personally*" (a sixty-year-old male liberal).

The General Conference data provide ample examples of how our circles of interaction influence our behavior. The survey included measures of region, age, gender, education, and income, which sociologists see as indicators of social structures that influence our patterns of social interaction.

First, let's look at how delegates differed in seeing some religious activity or event—worship, music, sermons, prayers—as the high point of the General Conference. Those in the Western Jurisdiction were more likely than those in any other jurisdiction to list religious aspects as the high point of the General Conference. Also, women, those who were older, those who had less education, and those with lower income were more likely to highlight religious experiences.

Turning now to delegates' desire for the UMC to "lead the way in finding solutions to public issues," about 93 percent do want the UMC to lead. Those from the Southeastern Jurisdiction, males, those with less education, and those with higher income are *less* likely to want the UMC to lead.

Let's take a more detailed look at views on the homosexuality issues. Overall, 54 percent of delegates *disagree* that homosexuality is a sin, 30 percent believe homosexual marriages should be permitted in the UMC, and 35 percent support ordination of homosexuals. Views on homosexuality vary widely across social circles. The most dramatic difference is by Jurisdiction:

Jurisdiction	Homosexuality Not Sin	Homosexual Marriage Permitted	Support for Ordination
Western	84%	64%	74%
North Central	61%	35%	45%
Northeastern	63%	37%	41%
South Central	55%	27%	33%
Southeastern	34%	14%	15%

Interpreted in the light of the logic presented above, delegates in the Western Jurisdiction, compared with those in the Southeastern Jurisdiction, would be far more likely to have conversations with persons who believe homosexuality is not a sin, who believe that homosexual marriages should be permitted, and who support ordination of homosexuals. It is important to note, however, that more than 34 percent of United Methodist lay members are in the Southeastern Jurisdiction and only about 5.5 percent in the Western Jurisdiction.[2]

Age differences on issues of homosexuality may give us a clue to their eventual resolution. Sociologist Karl Mannheim wrote, "That. . . youth lacks experience means a lightening of the ballast for the young; it facilitates their living on in a changing world." Delegates under fifty years of age were more liberal than those fifty and over on each of the three issues we have been considering. Sixty percent of those under age fifty *disagreed* with the statement, "Homosexuality is a sin," compared with 52 percent of those fifty and over. Thirty-eight percent of those under fifty agreed that homosexuals should be permitted to marry, compared with 26 percent of those fifty and over. And on the question of ordination, 45 percent of those under fifty favored ordination of homosexuals, compared to 31 percent of those fifty and older. In the general population of United Methodists, the differences between age groups are much sharper. The General Social Survey asked, "What about sexual relations between two adults of the same sex—do you think it is always wrong, almost always wrong, wrong only sometimes, or not wrong at all?" In 1996, 49 percent of United Methodists under the age of fifty responded "sometimes wrong" or "not wrong at all." Only 26 percent of those fifty and older gave these responses. Moreover, attitudes are changing rapidly: Nine years earlier, in 1987, 17 percent of those under fifty and 2 percent of those fifty and over gave these responses.

> The UMC is uniquely equipped to facilitate the enlarging of circles.

Gender and education are also indicators of networks of social relations. Looking to the future, the percentage of women delegates is likely to increase and the education level of delegates is likely to rise (along with that of the general population). How do gender and education affect delegates' views of the homosexuality issues? Women are more liberal on all three issues. Seventy-one percent of women, compared to 43 percent of men, disagree that homosexuality is a sin. Forty-five percent of women, compared to 19 percent of men, think the UMC should permit homosexual marriages. And women delegates are more likely (52 percent) than men (24 percent) to favor ordination of homosexuals.

Delegates with more formal education are also more liberal on all three issues. Those delegates with more than a bachelor's degree are more likely (59 percent) than those with a bachelor's degree or less (27 percent) to disagree that homosexuality is a sin. Thirty-three percent of those with more than a bachelor's would permit homosexual marriages, compared to 23 percent of those with a bachelor's or less. And 39 percent of those with more than a bachelor's favor ordination of homosexuals, compared to 26 percent of other delegates.

Finally, participation in organizations is an important aspect of one's social networks. Those delegates who attended some caucus meeting at the conference were more likely (39 percent) to favor ordaining homosexuals than those who did not (32 percent). But, of course, the caucus attended made all the difference! Eighty-three percent of those attending a meeting of the Methodist Federation of Social Action, but only 9 percent of those who attended a meeting of Good News, favor ordaining homosexuals.

The Uniqueness of The United Methodist Church

As discussed in chapter 2, the Wesleyan heritage drives us toward inclusiveness and diversity. The UMC is uniquely equipped to facilitate the enlarging of circles. Geographically the UMC is the most diverse of the large religious bodies in the United States. Until the recent decline of rural churches, the UMC had at least one local congregation in every *county* of the United States. Moreover, the representative delegate selection process assures that General Conference delegates reflect the denomination's geographical distribution. The UMC, the second largest Protestant body in the U.S., is far more geographically representative than the Southern Baptist Convention, the nation's largest Protestant body. I compared the proportion of delegates from each state to the 1988 Southern Baptist Convention and United Methodist Church General Conference with each state's proportion of representatives in the U.S. House of Representatives (which is determined by population distribution). The Methodist proportion is closer to the proportion of members in the U.S. House of Representatives in forty of the fifty states, and there are three ties. Moreover, Methodists, compared with Baptists, have far larger proportions of delegates from five of the six most populous states.

The UMC is also quite diverse socially. Sociologist N. J. Demerath, III, who highlights the importance of social heterogeneity, classifies Methodists as middle class, with an appreciable proportion of both upper class and, especially, lower class participants.[3] Based on more recent data, Wade Clark Roof and William McKinney give a similar characterization.[4]

There is also a great deal of diversity in the religious belief of the UMC. For example, our sample of U.S. delegates to the General Conference described themselves "in religious matters" as:

3%   Very conservative
47%   Conservative
46%   Liberal
4%   Very Liberal

Points of View

Apparently the diverse backgrounds of Methodists in fact lead to diverse points of view on homosexuality. Though most delegates (93 percent) think homosexuals should not be discriminated against in employment outside the church, delegates are more evenly divided on whether homosexuality is a sin (54 percent think it is not a sin), and whether the "ancient taboos" against homosexuality still apply (47 percent think they no longer apply). Most delegates do not want the church to ordain homosexuals (65 percent) or to allow homosexual marriages (70 percent), but more than one-fourth of the delegates do support these actions.[5]

Coming together for common purposes at the General Conference allows delegates to become close to people with opposing views. Fifty-eight delegates told me that something happened at General Conference that caused them to change their mind about homosexuality. Given the salience of the issue and the strong lobbying of delegates through the mail beginning long before the conference, it is not surprising that so few changed once they arrived at the conference. More than three-quarters (76 percent) of these delegates shifted to more acceptance of homosexuals. Influences on their becoming more accepting included conversations with other delegates, discussions in legislative committees, meeting gay and lesbian United Methodists, and some aspect of the plenary program or debates. Many of these delegates were also influenced positively by people or caucuses advocating for gays and lesbians or negatively by those on the other side.

Some delegates were influenced by references to the Bible. Witness this statement by a sixty-three-year-old delegate who considers herself very liberal in religious matters: "[One bishop's] words to our delegation that the Scriptures can be interpreted differently today than in days gone by firmed up my belief that homosexuals are born (created by

God) and could play an important role in the church by being ordained." A forty-eight-year-old delegate who describes himself as moderate in religious matters "softened" his position toward gays and lesbians after he "read a position paper that traced biblical history of homosexuality." Another moderate delegate, a forty-nine-year-old woman, became "more open" as she thought about another delegate's statement from the floor of the conference, "Jesus said nothing about homosexuality and neither should we."

It is interesting that a number of conservative delegates became more accepting of gays and lesbians. Here are some of their comments: One delegate in her fifties who considers herself a conservative said, "I was moved by the presenter on the social justice issue day. I continue to become more accepting as the issue becomes more personalized." Another conservative delegate, also in her fifties, "moderated" her opposition to accepting homosexuals after conversations with "those who have significant [gay and lesbian] ministries in their congregations." A forty-three-year-old delegate who considers herself conservative on religious matters was influenced by "the open door campaign and the fifteen bishops' statement." These made her "more open to learn about and understand gays and lesbians." A conservative delegate in his fifties said the "general tone of homosexual interaction made me more accepting of homosexuals." A forty-seven-year-old delegate who described himself as conservative on religious matters said the "witness event was very powerful. It made me rethink [my position] and hear other people's pain."

The statement by the fifteen bishops influenced several delegates. For example, a fifty-year-old delegate who describes himself as a moderate said that the statement of the fifteen bishops "made him aware that there are homosexuals that are excluded from being a part of the UMC." A fifty-five-year-old liberal delegate was energized by the stance of the fifteen bishops. "It caused me to go *very* public in the newspapers and elsewhere, defending the fifteen bishops. I had long taken that stance but now am very out front and public." Another liberal, a sixty-year-old man, had a similar experience: "The statement by the fifteen bishops gave me more courage to be forthright on the issue in my local setting."

Several delegates shifting to a less accepting position reacted negatively to the action of the fifteen bishops and the Open Door strategy of advocates for gays and lesbians. For example, a liberal delegate in her fifties said that "the action of the fifteen bishops [made her] angry and more conservative." A forty-nine-year-old man, a moderate, says that "the intense caucusing and the week of worship, which had an intense flavor of lobbying for 'Open Doors,' probably made me more hard-line than I intended to be going in, e.g., was not ready to specify 'self-avowed' or 'same-sex marriage' as bad, but the impact of the caucus and worship on me was a negative reaction."

Some of those delegates changing to a less accepting position were also influenced by contact with other delegates, especially the international delegates. A liberal delegate in her forties said, "Conversations with persons from different countries and cultures [convinced me] that the U.S. cannot dictate for the world." A fifty-five-year-old male delegate, also a liberal, said that opposition to homosexuality by delegates from Africa and from Mexico made him realize the implications of the issue for the global nature of the UMC.

Opening to the Holy Spirit

Enlarging our circles helps to open us to the leading of the Holy Spirit. Methodist historian Russell Richey asks, Can conference be again a means of grace?

To speak, as we have, of conference as a means of grace is to say that the Methodist genius has been to make structure serve its end; to conduct business in a gracious fashion; to orient Methodists out in mission and service to their neighborhood, community, and world; to establish its priorities through its rhythms; to orient in space and time to what had most gravity—namely the Holy Spirit.[6]

As we associate with people with different perspectives, our ideologies tend to dissolve so that we are more open to the Holy Spirit. Many delegates to the 1996 General Conference did sense the presence of the Holy Spirit in the civility of dialogue and the cordiality of fellowship.

The times of discernment encouraged by our bishops at the 1996 General Conference helped us enlarge our circles. Recall that the bishops urged the delegates "that each time you gather in a legislative committee, in a caucus meeting, in plenary, you begin with five minutes of reflecting with another person—perhaps someone you do not know well—speaking about these two questions: (1) What is my most earnest hope for the next few hours of this General Conference? (2) What do I believe is God's most fervent hope for these next few hours? Then we ask you to pray with that conversation partner beseeching God to bring the two hopes into one. We go to our discipline of intercessory prayer with confidence God will break in with energy, wisdom, and joy." This is a good illustration of how our leaders can help us enlarge our circles. But any local congregation can do this too so long as that congregation has sufficient diversity.

The biblical impetus for enlarging our circles of care and concern entails diversity at every possible level. That is why I would be wary of a recent suggestion by Lyle Schaller that the UMC should consider a structure that encourages

> The biblical impetus for enlarging our circles entails diversity at every possible level.

homogeneous annual conferences. Here are Schaller's examples of a possible structure:

> Thus, one annual conference might be composed of Korean and Korean-American congregations, another of reconciling congregations, a third of multicultural congregations, a fourth of large downtown churches, a fifth of small congregations served by bivocational ministers, a sixth of self-identified, theologically liberal churches, a seventh of congregations located in the same state or region, an eighth of self-identified evangelical congregations, and a ninth of Spanish language churches.[7]

I believe our biblical mandate is for facilitating interactions between and among the various categories of people and congregations listed by Schaller. His proposal appears to have the opposite effect. Though ethnic and language congregations may be justified, optimally, they would be sharing facilities or at least be yoked with other United Methodist congregations in the community. It appears more Christlike to strive, for example, for Reconciling Congregations that are accepting of Methodists with "transforming" views and Transforming Congregations that are accepting of those with "reconciling" views, than to put any structural barriers in the way of mutual understanding.

Undoubtedly we need further structural change (in addition to the significant flexibility already enacted at the 1996 General Conference). Fortunately the Connectional Process Team is taking its task seriously. But any changes should enhance rather than inhibit the opportunities to enlarge our circles, loosen the hold of culture on us, and open our lives to the Holy Spirit.

In time, talking about the Bible, opening our minds, and enlarging our circles will allow us to resolve our differences—but in the meantime it is critical to both our unity and our mission that we honor our agreements (chapter 6).

CHAPTER SIX
Honoring Our Agreements

The [editor] then stated categorically that the Methodist Publishing House could not desist from publishing articles persuasive of integrating the Church; that he could not even agree to give our side of the question equal space, or in fact, any space at all. He assigned as his reason for these decisions the fact that previous General Conferences of the Church had spoken, and he was carrying out the mandate of the Church in this regard. He gave us no comfort whatever.

These words are from a May 1961 bulletin of The Methodist Layman's Union. During the 1960s I compared the treatment of racial integration in the Sunday school literature of The Methodist Church and the Southern Baptist Convention. I suspected (correctly as it turns out) that there would be little difference in the personal views of editors in the two denominations. Because The Methodist Church had a much more connectional polity than the Southern Baptist Convention, however, I expected that the Methodist literature would be more supportive of racial integration. Even when the SBC passed relatively supportive resolutions about race relations, the chief editor kept reminding his staff that what they wrote had to be acceptable to the local congregations or they would be out of business. In contrast, once the General Conference of The Methodist Church mandated the promotion of racial integration, the chief Methodist editor strongly supported the literature staff's efforts to implement that mandate.

Polity makes a difference. This chapter considers the implications of our United Methodist connectional system for how we reach our agreements, how we implement those agreements, and how we live with our disagreements.

> Polity makes a difference.

Reaching Our Agreements

In Acts and the letters of Paul, we find the early church debating issues and reaching agreements. For example, in the fifteenth chapter of Acts we read that, "Paul and Barnabas and some of the others were appointed to go up to Jerusalem to discuss this question [must Gentiles be circumcised] with the apostles and the elders" (15:2). In Jerusalem the apostles and the elders listened to both sides, then, after much debate decided that Gentiles did not have to be circumcised and sent some of their number back to Antioch with Paul and Barnabas to inform Gentile Christians of their decision.

The United Methodist General Conference is a remarkable embodiment of representative democracy. UMC agreements are negotiated in a fair and orderly manner. Annual conference members are elected by local congregations. Those members, in turn, elect the delegates to the General Conference. UMC procedure and the presence of numerous caucus groups assure that the diversity of elements within the denomination fully participate in the selection of delegates. The UM *Discipline* sets legitimate, orderly procedures that assure that participants engage one another in genuine dialogue rather than simply trying to bull-

> The United Methodist General Conference is a remarkable embodiment of representative democracy.

doze through their opposition. Then the rules of the General Conference itself assure that various points of view are heard. Any local congregation or church member can send a petition to the General Conference. Then, during the first week of the two-week conference, every one of the thousands of petitions is carefully reviewed at least by one of the subcommittees within the ten legislative committees. Even if the committee votes overwhelmingly to accept or reject a petition, delegates on the minority side can still ask for the issue to be debated on the floor of the General Conference. Moreover, in the floor debates each side is assured of equal time to present its case. As a result most delegates (87 percent) perceived that the decision process in their legislative committees was fair and balanced, and most (82 percent) also thought that General Conference deliberations on public issues were characterized by honest, open dialogue. Specific to the issue of homosexuality, most delegates (77 percent) agreed that "My point of view on homosexuality was well represented at the General Conference." A smaller majority (57 percent) "thought the debate on homosexuality at the General Conference was fair and balanced." However, those who believe that "homosexuality is a sin" and those who do not were about equally likely to think the debate was fair and balanced.

Enforcing Our Agreements

There are strong mechanisms for enforcing our agreements. We have a strong polity that is anchored in the connection that requires a trust clause in deeds to local property and deploys clergy by episcopal appointment to local churches. Other elements of the polity include the system of interaction in conferences, the communication network, the pension system, the publications, and a deep sense of loyalty to the denomination by many of its members. Two recent cases demonstrate the strength of our polity. First, consider the much publicized trial of the Reverend Jimmy Creech who, in September 1997, performed a covenanting service uniting two women. Charges were brought that he had violated church rules, with special reference to the Social Principles statement, "Ceremonies that celebrate homosexual unions shall not be conducted by our ministers and shall not be conducted in our Churches." Once charges were brought and validated by the Committee on Investigation of the Nebraska Annual Conference, Creech was suspended from his position as pastor of the First United Methodist Church in Omaha. At his trial in March 1998 Creech offered as a principal part of his defense that the Social Principles are not binding law. Though this argument apparently did not convince the majority of the thirteen clergy members of the Nebraska Annual Conference serving as jurors, Creech escaped conviction because the *Discipline* requires at least nine votes to convict and only eight jurors voted for conviction. As a consequence of the acquittal, Creech's suspension was lifted and he resumed his duties in Omaha. As we will see, there is much more to this story; but had the story ended here, we would already have a clear insight into the strength of UMC polity. Creech came within one vote of the possibility of losing his credentials as a United Methodist minister. The trial, by underscoring the mechanisms by which the UMC can enforce the will of the General Conference should certainly give pause to any minister contemplating actions contrary to that will.

As it turns out, a number of things happened in the aftermath of the trial. For one thing, just before the meetings of the Nebraska Annual Conference in June, Nebraska's Bishop Joel Martinez, exercising his right to appoint ministers, decided not to reappoint Creech to the

Omaha church, giving Creech the choice of accepting another appointment in Nebraska, seeking an appointment in another annual conference, or taking a leave of absence. Creech decided to take a leave of absence. Meanwhile, the bishops of the South Central Jurisdiction requested the Judicial Council to rule on the legal status of the Social Principles; and once the Judicial Council agreed to do so, the Council of Bishops issued a statement in which they agreed to uphold the *Discipline*, including the Social Principles while waiting for a decision. In August the Judicial Council ruled that the prohibition against homosexual unions does have the status of church law. Though this ruling did not affect the Creech case, it did raise the stakes for any minister considering conducting a ceremony celebrating a homosexual union. Indeed, only a few months later, in March 1999, a UMC trial court found the Reverend Greg Dell "guilty of disobedience to the order and discipline of the United Methodist Church" for conducting a ceremony celebrating the union of two male members of the church he pastors, Broadway United Methodist Church in Chicago. Meanwhile, in California, formal complaints were brought against sixty-eight of the 150 UMC clergy members who, in January 1999, participated in a "holy union" service, uniting two women leaders in the California-Nevada Annual Conference.

A recent case in the California-Nevada Annual Conference illustrates the role of the trust clause and denominational ownership of local church property in our strong polity. Believing their understanding of evangelical theology was at odds with the conference leadership, eighteen clergy and twenty-five lay persons called for "outside mediation to establish a just process for evangelical pastors and churches to retain their local property with some just compensation to the Conference." Some of these persons later asked for a separate "evangelical" district or conference. When the conference did not grant these requests, one congregation decided to leave the UMC. Possibly in an attempt to circumvent UMC polity, the congregation's trustees remained members of the UMC to discharge their responsibilities as trustees, and subsequently leased the property to the new church for a nominal amount. However, exercising its legal control under church law, the conference claimed the property, then sold it to the new church and placed most of the proceeds in a fund for starting new United Methodist churches.

North Georgia Conference Bishop G. Lindsey Davis's response to acts of protest by the First United Methodist Church in Marietta, Georgia, illustrates the exercise of control based both on the trust clause and on the appointive power of the bishop. However, Bishop Davis appears to understand that, though the strength of the formal polity provides a context that facilitates the resolution of issues, the hard work of resolving issues is a part of the ongoing relationships within the community of faith. In March, 1998, after the Board of Stewards of this large church voted to "redirect" funds they should have paid for churchwide programs of the UMC, Davis said, "We work in a web of intricate connections, and part of our understanding of what it means to be a community of faith is to be involved in that kind of connection. To go off on your own, so to speak, flies in the face of our polity, discipline and order."[1]

As the controversy continued, Bishop Davis announced in March, 1999, that the Reverend Charles Sineath, the senior pastor who had served the church for twenty-two years, would be reassigned. Sineath chose to retire rather than be reappointed, and subsequently agreed to pastor a new congregation, not affiliated with The United Methodist Church, formed by a significant minority of the members of First Church.[2] Though this loss of members is certainly regrettable, the fact that First Church will remain a vital congregation within the UMC is due in large part to the strength of our polity. An important consequence of this polity is that, once a congregation has reached the point of wanting to leave the UMC, it cannot leave precipitously. The process allows time for sober second thought by both parties. The United Methodist polity is connectional, not congregational.

Ministering to the World

Through our system we secure and deploy resources throughout the world. The connectional system holds together a vital structure of social action. Here is how it was described by the bishops in their report of the Global Nature of the United Methodist Church:

> Connectionalism in the United Methodist tradition is multi-leveled, global in spread, and local in thrust.
> We are connected by sharing a common tradition of faith.
> We are connected by sharing together a constitutional polity, including a leadership of general superintendence [i.e., the episcopacy].
> We are connected by sharing a common mission which we seek to carry out together both globally and locally.
> We are connected organizationally in and through conferences that reflect both the inclusive and representative character of our fellowship.
> We share a common ethos which characterizes our distinctive way of doing things.
> We are connected by a common journey of more fully expressing our connectionalism from the local to the global and from the global to the local.
> For us connectionalism is not merely a linking of one connectional charge conference to another horizontally across the globe. It is, rather, a vital web of interactive and intertwining relationships that enables us to express freely,

justly, and in dignity at both global and local levels our essential identity, inclusive fellowship, common mission, distinctive ethos, and visible unity.[3]

Recall from chapter 2 the words of Bishop Arthur Kulah from war-torn Liberia: "Without your prayers, without your support, without your cooperation, our annual conference wouldn't have been where it is today."

The connectional system helps to focus our ministry on more universal concerns—those that go beyond our immediate circles of social class and region. It is important to understand that though delegates were intensely lobbied by those for whom homosexual issues were their primary concern, homosexual issues were not the *primary* concern for most delegates. As reported in chapter 2, when we asked delegates, "Considering everything, what stands out as the high point of the 1996 General Conference for you?" they responded with a wide range of issues and actions. More than 40 percent of the delegates responding to this question listed either the inspirational speech of Hillary Rodham Clinton or that of Bishop Arthur Kulah. For about one-fourth of them the highlight was the conference's emphasis on spirituality, discernment, worship, and prayer. Global representation at the conference and the global nature of the church were highlights for nearly one-third of the delegates. In fact, for the vast majority of delegates the highlight of the General Conference was not related to a highly controversial issue. Activities related to the issue of homosexuality were the highlight for only 5 percent of the delegates.

> The connectional system is a vital structure of social action.

The strength of polity is especially crucial when, ministering to the world, we must challenge entrenched social structures. The example of promoting racial justice through our Sunday school literature shows why we must retain a strong polity. Our strong polity allowed the general church to be a leader in some aspects of the civil rights movement; for example, providing integrated pictures in Sunday school materials long before commercial advertisers felt free to use such pictures. More recently our strong polity has facilitated the ordination and appointment of women clergy.

Living with Our Disagreements

The UMC connection consists of the continually negotiated agreements that govern our lives together. We are all better off when these agreements are honored voluntarily. Our strong polity is best used as a framework for education and persuasion. For example, the property arrangement discussed earlier best serves its purpose when, knowing the difficulty of leaving, leaders of congregations work harder at reconciling differences. And leaders at all levels have an obligation not only to educate those who disagree but also to listen to them carefully enough that any legitimate concerns will find their way into the process by which agreements are assessed and, often, renegotiated.

When we continue to disagree, we treat each other civilly—in the spirit of Christ. We affirm the worth of others and have cordial conversations with them. And we live by the agreements we have even while educating and persuading others as a basis for new agreements.

For one thing we affirm the worth of opponents and continue to listen to them. Witness the Methodist editor discussed at the beginning of this chapter. He did take a very strong stand against resisters, but then he impressed upon his editors the full extent of the resistance, requesting them to keep all these things in mind in case they should be relevant to editorial policy. Here is one of his communications to the editors:

Perhaps you are aware that I went to a meeting at Alexandria, La., where hearings on the church school literature and on the position of The Methodist Church about various social questions were held. At this time the attached documents were presented to the committee from [two local churches]. It is indispensable that each of you be clearly aware of the contents of these papers, especially the sections that bear on the curriculum materials which you personally produce, both because they represent a large segment of Methodist sentiment and because they reveal that we very often do not communicate our basic intentions in some of the material we edit.[4]

The editor-in-chief allowed his editors freedom yet wanted them to be aware of the total context in which they exercise that freedom. This wise policy resulted in effective promotion of racial justice in the Methodist literature.

During plenary sessions at the 1992 General Conference in Louisville, there were sharp differences with emotions sometimes running high; and the bishops presiding over the proceedings continually reminded the body of the tone they intended for the discussion to take. For example, when one delegate made a proposal that many interpreted as a means of short-circuiting the discussion of homosexuality and was promptly rebuked by another delegate (who drew applause from his supporters), the bishop presiding over that session intervened:

All right now, sisters and brothers, let me interrupt [the speaker] just a moment. This is the family of God at work. We're not trying to win or to lose, we're trying to discern together the will of God. And I trust that we will refrain from applause in order that we may build one another up in love and hold one another up in prayer.[5]

Despite sharp differences on this emotion-charged issue, the debates on homosexuality were civil and productive.

Two of the reasons for this civility were the rules of order and procedures built into the UMC polity and the fact that Methodists despite their diversity have a number of beliefs, traditions, and loyalties in common. Not the least of these is Wesley's own thought and example. In a letter to a friend in 1765, Wesley makes plain his reliance on people's Christian experience rather than their theological opinions. He tells how he and his brother Charles thirty years ago, thought "it our duty to oppose Predestination with our whole strength: not as an opinion, but as a dangerous mistake." Yet "Mr. H——— and Mr. N——— hold this, and yet I believe these have real Christian experience. But if so, this is only an opinion: it is not subversive (here is clear proof to the contrary) of the very foundation of Christian experience."

Ninety-eight percent of my sample agreed that "I am willing to be friends with a UMC member whose opinion on homosexuality is different from my own." And 83 percent reported that they had actually "had cordial conversations with delegates whose opinions were opposite of [their] own regarding homosexuality."

I experienced a startling moment while observing the Council of Bishops meeting in Lincoln, Nebraska. Following the opening communion service (on Sunday, April 26, 1998), I was coming out of St. Paul UMC with several bishops and their spouses. As we came out to the street, we suddenly realized that we were surrounded by a large group of people holding signs. For a split second my mind turned to the hate signs I had seen on television during the trial of Jimmy Creech. Soon I realized that this group was not full of hate, but of concern. These loyal United Methodists had come by car, van, and bus from throughout Nebraska to tell their bishops to uphold the UMC's ban on the celebration of homosexual unions. They were an orderly group with signs that expressed their view forcefully, but respectfully. As it turned out their view prevailed not only in a statement by the Council of Bishops to uphold and administer the *Discipline* of the church but also in a subsequent decision by the Judicial Council that the ban on celebration of homosexual unions has the force of law. But regardless of how those decisions went or what decisions will be made about this issue in the future, these loyal United Methodists exemplified the orderly civil process of our connection.[6]

As the title of this chapter implies, I think we are all well served by honoring our agreements. Even when we intensely disagree with existing agreements, I think we are all better off by honoring the agreements at the same time that we voice our dissent and work actively to change them. Two bishops involved in the recent cases discussed above exemplified this principle. Bishop C. Joseph Sprague in Northern Illinois and Bishop Melvin Talbert in California-Nevada filed complaints against pastors performing same-sex unions, but expressed their own belief that the church laws they were enforcing should be changed.

> Even when we disagree, we are better off by honoring our agreements even while we work to change them.

Bishop Talbert stated: "I will uphold the law, but I will not be silenced. I will continue speaking out against the law and will continue working to change the position of our church to be more in keeping with the teachings and compassion of Jesus."[7] Having made clear that I think we are all better off in the long run when we honor our agreements, I must add that United Methodists have collectively agreed to respect civil disobedience. Though we must enforce our agreements, a part of our way of living with our disagreements is to treat civilly even those who on principle are compelled to dishonor our agreements. We not only treat them civilly but use their acceptance of the consequences as occasions to search our own hearts, bearing in mind that sometimes these passionate dissenters are eventually proved right. Yet the civil disobedient also should be civil and are not relieved from the duty to think whether their actions may delay the time their view may prevail. History will judge all of us not only by whether our intentions were pure and our cause just but also by whether our actions indeed helped or hindered that cause.

My statistical analysis related a measure of civility to several variables that are possible indicators of delegates' opportunities to open their minds and enlarge their circles of caring and concern. These variables were education, gender, age, previous involvement at the regional or national level of the UMC, years in the UMC, whether clergy or laity, and income. Two examples from the ten-item civility scale are: "I had cordial conversations with delegates whose opinions were opposite my own regarding homosexuality"; and "It is important that the General Conference decisions reflect the diversity within our denomination." As it turns out, the only statistically significant predictor of civility in my analysis was gender. Women were more civil than men. This finding may reflect persistent differences in the socialization of females and males in our society. However, it is not surprising that women play a critical role in generating civility on controversial issues within the General Conference. This finding may reflect the fact that United Methodist women have a tradition of "mission" studies in which, in their local and regional groups, they do serious study of the major issues facing the society and the church. For example, such studies in the 1950s and 1960s and the quiet leadership of the women who participated in them were crucial influences in preparing the church for racial integration.

We all benefit by honoring our agreements. It is perilous to dishonor present agreements rather than engage in the education and persuasion that may bring about new ones.

Educating and persuading means staying in touch, taking into account the views of others. Though connection is always being negotiated and education and persuasion is a continuous process, we must honor our agreements lest we erode our polity and impede our mission. Our leaders must inspire us to honor our agreements, even as they teach us that it is once more time for Methodists to lead (chapter 7).

Chapter Seven
A Time to Lead

"[The Methodists] made the conception of the brotherhood of [all people] and of the importance of [all people], a vivid reality. They had produced the final effective force which hereafter made slavery impossible among progressive races."

This extraordinary compliment to Methodism comes from the philosopher Alfred North Whitehead in his book, *Adventures of Ideas.*[1]

Methodists have been leaders in effecting dramatic advances in society. Methodists today still want their church to provide leadership for our society. For example, 83 percent of the 1996 General Conference delegates agreed that "The UMC should lead the way in finding solutions to public issues."

> Methodists have been leaders in effecting dramatic advances in society.

Whitehead held that "the Methodist movement succeeded because it came at the right time." According to Whitehead, "the final introduction of a reform does not necessarily prove the moral superiority of the reforming generation....Conditions may have changed, so that what is possible now may not have been possible" earlier. Among the conditions that may have changed he listed "the gradual growth of the requisite communal customs" that could sustain the reform.[2]

Culture Change

As suggested in chapter 3, viewing changes in our culture in the light of what the Bible tells us about God at work in the world helps us discern God's contemporary revelation. Changes in at least two of the communal customs of U.S. society set the stage for Methodists to lead again. Biblical literalism is declining, and acceptance of homosexuality is increasing. These changes present a challenge to Methodists. Increasing general education and knowledge of biblical scholarship have contributed to a steady decline in those who say the Bible is to be taken literally. Polls show, for example, that the percent of Americans who believe the Bible is to be taken literally has declined from 39 percent in 1983 to 31 percent in 1995.[3] Among United Methodists during a similar period, 1984 to 1998, belief that the Bible should be taken literally declined from 35 percent to 26 percent. The challenge is to assure that our society, in rejecting biblical literalism, does not reject the Bible. This challenge is increased by the fact that, even as biblical literalism is declining, its influence in the political world appears to be increasing.[4] We must be vigilant against misleading use of the Bible in public discourse, and we must not let those turned off by this political misuse of the Bible be turned off to biblical faith. Fortunately our Methodist heritage of open-minded biblical interpretation provides rich resources for facing this challenge to lead people and societies to a culturally aware biblical faith.

In a related but, as we will see, somewhat independent trend, Americans are becoming more accepting of homosexuals. More than twenty years ago Letha Scanzoni and Virginia Ramey Mollenkott wrote a moving and spiritually profound book, *Is the Homosexual My Neighbor?*[5] They argued that the time had come for the church not only to recognize homosexual persons as children of God but also to allow their full participation within the church. But for me, as for most of the people I knew then, the time had not come. As a sociologist I was well aware of homosexual persons in an unhealthy and morally degrading lifestyle, but I was not aware that I knew respected professionals and other responsible persons in the community who were homosexuals. I certainly had not met any same-sex couples with committed relationships who, as a couple, were playing a positive and responsible role in the community. Much has changed in twenty years. Many people in our society, myself among them, have enlarged their circle of coworkers, neighbors, and friends to include persons who are respected in their occupations and professions and in the community and are homosexual persons. Most Americans are aware that persons prominent in the business and political world as well as in music and the arts are homosexual persons. Just how far this acceptance has gone can be seen in business corporations' personnel and marketing policies, on the Internet, and in advice columns, such as Ann Landers; but most of all in responses to national polls. Opinion polls reflect the changing attitudes resulting from increased association with homosexual persons and the resulting understanding of homosexuality. Recent polls show, for example, that 61 percent of Americans (71 percent of those aged eighteen to twenty-nine) think high school education courses should not "tell students that homosexuality is immoral." Forty-four percent (57 percent of those aged eighteen to twenty-nine) think that "homosexuality is a way of life that should be accepted by society." Forty-four percent also hold that homosexuality is either wholly (33 percent) or partly (11 percent) something a person is born with. As discussed in chapter 4, the 1994 General Social Survey showed that 53 percent of United Methodists believe that sexual orientation is something an individual cannot change. Forty-nine percent of Americans agreed that "Love between homosexual partners can be just as real as love between a man and a woman" (25 percent disagreed, 26 percent were unsure). And, specific to one of the issues of this book, a

1996 Gallup Poll shows that the majority of Americans (53 percent) think homosexual persons should have equal opportunities for clergy jobs.

As people learn more about homosexuality and encounter coworkers, friends, and loved ones who are homosexual, their perceptions change. One delegate made my point explicitly by writing in the margin of his questionnaire that both he and his wife have siblings who are homosexuals. This trend is reflected in the fact that the majority of the 1996 delegates do not believe that homosexuality is a sin. Fifty-six percent said they had become "more accepting of gays and lesbians" over the previous four years. But it is not just delegates who are becoming more accepting of gay and lesbian persons. As discussed earlier, one series of biennial national polls suggests that acceptance of same-sex relationships increased dramatically among United Methodists in recent years. For example, in 1994 19 percent of United Methodists said sexual relations between two adults of the same sex is "wrong only sometimes, or not wrong at all." Just two years later, in 1996 (and again in 1998), the percentage had more than doubled to about 39 percent.[6]

God Calls The United Methodist Church

Clearly the "communal customs" of American society are changing in ways that can sustain a new acceptance of homosexual persons. Whitehead referred to social conditions that made the time ripe. In faith, we can see the God of the Bible in such changing social conditions. God is calling Methodists to demonstrate the reconciling power of the Bible through our resolution of the issue of homosexuality and to lead our society to an informed understanding of how the Bible bears on issues like homosexuality.

One of my seminary professors taught, "where the

world's needs and your talents meet, there is your call." This variant of the biblical, "of [them] to whom much is given much is also required," suggests that for individuals and institutions God calls us where our specific capabilities match the concrete needs of the world in our time. It is time for us to lead because once more events and forces have created a situation in which the world's needs and Methodism's talents meet.

There is the need for the organized onslaught against the rights of homosexual persons to be countered by the institutional weight of the church. As United Methodists we have affirmed our commitment to champion the civil rights of homosexual persons. And we have many resources—prayer, publishing, lobbying, local church actions—available to us in honoring this commitment.

Our society needs more situations that open minds and enlarge circles of friendship. The intense relationships in legislative committees and other activities at General Conferences and the various dialogues and studies in annual conferences and local congregations provide many such situations.

There is the need of those homosexual persons who know they have no choice of sexual orientation to be assured that God did not make a mistake—to know that God intends them to have the fullest expression of human happiness. And there is the need for them to know that such happiness for all persons entails strict moral standards of fidelity and mutual love. This affirmation is already available in many UMC congregations.

> Christians need not choose between their intuitive predisposition to acceptance and their faithfulness to the Bible.

There is the need for the loved ones and associates of such persons to know that they do not have to choose between their intuitive Christian predisposition to acceptance and their faithfulness to the Bible. Polls suggest that Americans are more ready to accept homosexuality than they are to believe that God accepts it! For example, a 1992 national poll showed that 60 percent of those surveyed agreed with the statement, "Homosexuality is against God's law." Yet only 30 percent agreed that "Homosexuality is wrong and there should be laws against it." Another poll, noted above, showed that 61 percent (71 percent of those eighteen through twenty-nine) thought high school education courses should not "tell students that homosexuality is immoral." Many people are by intuition more accepting than they think the Bible is. Who better than Methodists can teach people that they can be accepting of homosexual persons as a part of their affirmation of biblical faith? And if we tell people it is because of the Bible that we accept homosexuals, they may begin to look at the Bible in a different light. Here more than at any other point our distinctive talent meets the world's needs. Because we Methodists make the Bible primary in our faith and life, yet approach the Bible with minds open to understanding it in its cultural context, we are in a position to meet the critical need of the world today to experience the power of the God of the Bible.

Many see conflict between Jesus' teachings and some conservatives' view of homosexuals. In the first assignment in my Sociology of Religion course, students are asked to describe the social relationships that sustain one of their beliefs. One student, in explaining why he believes that homosexuality is wrong, recounted sermons his pastor had preached and the Bible passages the pastor quoted. The pastor drew the conclusion that Christians should not associate with homosexuals. I was a bit surprised to read in a later essay by this same student that a lesbian couple was among his best friends. When he came in to talk about the essay, I told him of my surprise. "But Professor Wood," he said, "that same pastor introduced me to Jesus who loves everyone and accepts everyone."

Our society's move in the direction of acceptance of homosexual persons is an opportunity for biblical witness that applies biblical morality to emerging relationships. But let's be clear that we do not take our cues solely from the culture. Our understanding of our culture must be part of our dialogue about the Bible and part of our watching for the Holy Spirit. For example, there is no doubt that most Americans, including most Christians, travel in circles that are permeated with materialism and, specifically, consumerism. But nothing in the Bible would support the thought that God is calling us to this kind of consumerism rather than "laying up for ourselves treasures in heaven." Specifically on sexual matters, a decision to have a child out of wedlock is now accepted by the majority of Americans. Yet this trend raises serious moral questions for biblical Christians, including its relation to the critical problem of children in poverty.

> Our understanding of our culture must be part of our dialogue about the Bible.

In contrast, as our discussions about the changing roles of homosexual persons in our society and changing views of homosexuality in our culture become conversations about the Bible, we see that much of the example and teaching of Jesus are congruent with acceptance. Early Jewish Christians learned through experience that Christ accepted and vitalized the lives of Gentile Christians without their accepting all of the Jewish laws and practices (for example, circumcision). The early church's encounters with Gentiles may be instructive for us today (see especially Acts, chapters 9 through 11). As societal and cultural changes brought the church in contact with people of diverse backgrounds, the leadership's assumption that Christ came only to the Jews was shaken. Peter reluctantly accepted Cornelius' invitation to tell him about Christ. And, "when the Holy Spirit came upon all who were listening to the message," those "who had come with Peter were astonished that the gift of the Holy Spirit should have been poured out even on Gentiles" (NEB). Upon his return to Jerusalem, Peter had to answer to the church leadership for his association with the "uncircumcised." But Peter persuaded them that because the Gentiles had received the gift of the Holy Spirit, they must be accepted into the church. This same test of membership—the gift of the Holy Spirit—was then applied by the church leaders when they heard that in Antioch pagans were becoming believers in the Lord Jesus. Barnabas, whom they sent to investigate, rejoiced when he "saw the divine grace at work." Again and again throughout Acts we read of the Holy Spirit trumping the law as the church reaches beyond Judaism.[7]

Perhaps we will learn through our experience of Christ's working in the lives of homosexual persons. Last year I met a gay couple who had been loyal and committed to each other for several years. Since I knew the grandfather of one of these men, I asked him whether that grandfather had accepted the relationship. "Not at first," he told me. "But then I made some serious mistakes and got into a bit of trouble. As granddaddy observed how John stood by me and helped me straighten out my life—then his attitude changed." The more I learned of how this particular couple built each other up in love, the more I was able to understand those who believe that such unions can pass the test of biblical morality. I do believe God's Holy Spirit was at work in their lives together. Our challenge is to accept homosexual persons while holding up for them the biblical standard of fidelity in relationships and responsibility in the community.

I was struck by a poignant letter to the editor of *The United Methodist Reporter* in the wake of the verdict in the Jimmy Creech trial. A pastor writes about Ray, "a godly man" who "loves the Lord and his church. Ray has been a Methodist Christian for decades." The letter continues, "Ray appeared at my office door with a disconcerted look

on his face. He said, 'Would you tell me where in the Bible
it says we should marry two lesbians?' My heart dropped
as I realized that he had heard about the Creech incident.
My mind began to scramble for the right words that might
ease Ray's mind. Unfortunately none came. Ray started
walking toward the door, he paused and looked back to
me. He slowly shook his head and said, 'I'm ashamed to
call myself a United Methodist.' "[8]

My heart goes out to Ray and the many like him. By
neglecting our Wesleyan heritage in approaching the
Bible, we have let him down. This pastor apparently
shared Ray's view; but even if he had wanted to ease
Ray's mind by showing him how biblical Christians can
think it possible for some same-sex unions to pass the test
of biblical morality, he probably could not have done so.
Ray had been allowed for too many years to hold a literalistic view of the Bible. What a difference culturally aware
Bible study groups can make. In a recent group meeting
the leader began by telling us the stories of two couples in
churches he had pastored. One couple of young professionals had befriended an inner-city mother and her children. They provided food for the family, and they also
tutored the children in their school work. The other couple
had over the years received into their home numerous foster children—troubled teenagers who were hard for the
state to place elsewhere. The first couple was two gay
men, the second was two lesbians. Both couples were in
committed, responsible relationships. After telling these
stories, the leader then led us through each of the passages
in the Bible that refer to homosexuals. In each case we
looked at the passage in context, then the leader asked us
to consider whether these passages were relevant to the
couples we had discussed. As we talked about the Bible in
this way, we all gained new insight into the issue of homosexuality. Most did not think these passages applied to the

couples who built one another up in a Christlike love that overflowed into the surrounding community. Just as important, those who felt the passages did apply expressed a new understanding of how sincere biblical Christians could disagree on this issue. Mutual understanding that those on both sides of this issue accept the authority and experience the power of the Bible is the key to resolving our crisis over biblical authority.

> We must see that those on both sides of the homosexuality issue accept the authority and experience the power of the Bible.

More such Bible studies like the one described might stem the tide of Americans who are rejecting biblical faith because of misunderstandings about the Bible. One Episcopal bishop observes that "Many former churchgoers have simply given up on Christianity. . . . They don't believe that the literal readings of the Scripture can solve the complex social and ethical issues of our day."[9] As Methodists, with our Wesleyan approach to the Bible, face the homosexuality issue in all its complexity, we may learn afresh how the God of the Bible is at work in the world. And we can take up the challenge to lead contemporary people and societies to a biblical faith that, interpreting the Bible in the light of the culture of its authors, becomes open to the living word of the God of the Bible who speaks to us in our culture today.

Signs of Waking

The church as a whole can lead only after some within it awaken to what God is doing in the contemporary world. For example, as I recalled above, in the 1950s and 1960s the teaching materials and discussions of Methodist women's "schools of mission" began to prepare the way for racial integration in the South before the secular society (and before many of the male church leaders) were ready to accept it. Today there are many signs of United Methodists awaking and listening for God's call. Here are a few of those signs.

Clearly the Committee to Study Homosexuality, which reported to the 1992 General Conference, met the living Christ in their efforts to understand how God's word helps us resolve the issue of homosexuality. Though, ultimately, this diverse set of United Methodists was not successful in reaching a common understanding, their report formed the basis of excellent study materials for local churches. Perhaps even more important, their mutual acceptance of one another evident in their dialogue became a model for the church. The spirit of the study committee is illuminated by a widely circulated story about the committee's deliberations.

> The moment was unforgettable. United Methodist layman William Lux of Manchester, Iowa, was struggling to express his deeply held beliefs that homosexual practice is contrary to Christian teaching. When he proposed words to be added to the final report of the Committee to Study Homosexuality, the Rev. Tex Sample of Kansas City, Mo., an outspoken advocate for the acceptance of gays and lesbians, jumped in quickly.
>
> "I don't think you want to say that, Bill, because I don't think it represents your position strongly enough," Dr. Sample said. "What I think you want to say is that homosexual practice is contrary to Christian teaching because it contradicts God's expressed will for human good."
>
> Those in the meeting room . . . broke into gales of appreciative laughter at the irony of one advocate helping an advocate of an opposing position express his viewpoint.[10]

This spirit proved contagious. The deliberations of the Church and Society legislative committee, which I observed in Louisville and especially in Denver, were permeated by this same spirit, with its implication that different views of the Bible are accepted as sincere. The story that began chapter 5 is but one example.

Other signs of waking to God's call are the new understandings and associations that resulted from local church studies based on the material prepared by the Committee to Study Homosexuality. Twenty of us in St. Mark's UMC (Bloomington, Indiana) participated in a six-evening study of homosexuality, based on the UMC materials. We held a wide range of views on homosexuality, but all were moved by the testimony of a mother of a gay teenage boy.

Here is how our pastor reported the event in his sermon the following Sunday:

> The family that visited us last Tuesday was very open, very loving, and very Christian. The mother was especially well versed in the Scriptures. She told about the time two years ago when her then-fourteen-year-old son talked with her about knowing that he was homosexual. . . . She told us how, after her son had gone to school the next day, she cried and cried. "All I could think about were the many hateful stereotypes that I had been taught about homosexuals," she said. . . . "But after several hours of crying and praying, God whispered to me. God said, 'You have always known that you have a wonderful son. You still have a wonderful son.' "
>
> [Then she said] "In a photograph I was looking at the face of my son whom I loved and I decided that rather than allow the hateful stereotypes I'd previously been taught about homosexuality to disfigure the face of my son, I would place the face of my son over the stereotypes I had been taught about homosexuality. I decided to let him give me new understanding of homosexuality, rather than allowing what I'd heard about homosexuality to change my love and respect for him."[11]

The fifteen bishops who in Denver dissented from UMC policies on homosexuality are also a sign of waking.

Though only about half the delegates reacted positively to the action of these bishops, and some of these bishops have told me they would have done things a bit differently if they had it to do over, they set the church as a whole on a course of healthy discussions about homosexuality. One such discussion was within the Council of Bishops, meeting in Lincoln in the spring of 1998. The bishops released a pastoral letter making clear that they would honor the church's agreements even as those agreements are being renegotiated.

As an observer of the General Commission on Christian Unity and Interreligious Concerns' Theological Diversity Dialogues, I saw a set of diverse Methodists listening for God's call. Circles were enlarged and perspectives broadened. And the paper written by the group, "In Search of Unity," has spawned many productive dialogues within the UMC. These dialogues may well not have taken place had the fifteen bishops not made their statement. At any rate, two of those bishops were among the participants in the dialogues.

Perhaps the most dramatic dialogue based on the "In Search of Unity" document was the one held at the 1998 Nebraska Annual Conference. Dr. Kent Millard, who moderated the dialogue for the nearly one thousand clergy and laity, described it this way: "Rev. Jimmy Creech was sitting beside the pastors who had taken him to trial, and the atmosphere was tense. The high degree of anxiety in this group was obvious."

Those who wanted to speak were given two minutes "to simply share their own life journey." After each speaker there was a time of silence and then a verse of a hymn. "It was conducted in a context of respect and worship. And it was very reconciling because we began to listen to one another." "The testimonials shared—no matter from which perspective—came from the heart and a strong sense of conviction."[12] Several other annual conferences found creative ways to treat the homosexuality issue in the 1998 sessions. For example, California-Pacific Conference avoided the labels of "reconciling" and "transforming" and voted to become a "welcoming" conference, open to all regardless of sexual orientation. Several conferences deferred or tabled resolutions related to sexual orientation and planned dialogues, pulpit exchanges, and other means toward better understanding of the various views on the issue of homosexuality.[13]

All of these are signs that we are beginning to recognize the spiritual unity that underlies our different views on homosexuality. This is an atmosphere conducive to United Methodists hearing God's call to lead people and societies to a culturally aware biblical faith. But there is a need for leaders who will articulate that call. That is why one of the greatest signs of hope for the UMC is the spiritual awakening evident within the Council of Bishops. As often happens with the working of the Holy Spirit, the precise nature of this spiritual awakening is hard to discern. Yet several bishops have spoken to me about the way they have begun to pray together in small groups and to talk more openly and earnestly about their differences. My sense is that over the past decade many bishops have been quiet leaders in this awakening. Powerful sermons by three southern bishops were dramatic public manifestations of the emergence of spiritual leadership among the bishops. Taken together the sermons by Bishop Joe Pennel, Bishop Ray Chamberlain, and Bishop Janice Huie clearly depicted the church as a vehicle of God's grace in the midst of the issues and controversies affecting contemporary people and societies. They sharply underscored the necessity for honoring our agreements and discussing our disagreements openly and with the spirit of Christ. They strongly affirmed the authority of the Bible and the important roles of reason, experience, and tradition in discerning God's living word. Most dramatically, they galvanized their fellow bishops with the call to a biblically based shepherd's role in ministering to all who are touched by the crisis over homosexuality.

At their meeting in Lincoln, Nebraska, the bishops were forging a statement to the church in the aftermath of the acquittal of the Reverend Jimmy Creech. In his sermon there Bishop Joe Pennel did not mention the issue of homosexuality, but he talked about how the early church approached decisions in the midst of their struggles with opposing views and differing theologies. He spoke of these early Christians' practice of hospitality toward each other, their forthright debates, their use of scripture to support what they believed, their prayer and discernment about the issues, their telling the stories of the work of the Holy Spirit, and their giving theological reasons for their various standpoints. Bishop Pennel challenged the Council of Bishops to model this kind of decision making for the UMC so that the Holy Spirit can lead us in the contemporary world.

At the next meetings of the bishops, at Simpsonwood, Bishop Ray Chamberlain continued the theme of Christian decision making:

> Let me illustrate how we Methodists generally work with the application of our beliefs to our laws—and rules. We accept the basic premise of the sufficiency of Scripture for salvation and practice. We interpret Scripture through *tradition, reason* and *experience.* . . .
>
> Let's use some scales to illustrate my point. [He had balance scales, a Bible, and symbols of tradition, reason, and experience.]
>
> Take, for example, homosexuality. How do we determine what our rule will be?
>
> Well, the Scriptures speak against it—add weights.
>
> Tradition weighs in against it—add weights.

To balance that out we need what I will call warrants—some determinants to outweigh Scripture and tradition. Obviously, our denomination has not felt comfortable with the weight of warrants to counterbalance the weight of Scripture. So, that's how we arrive at our current position on homosexuality. It's so easy, isn't it? Just take the Scriptures at face value.

So, why all the uproar?

Let's look at another issue: slavery. The Scriptures seem to allow for slavery—add weights.

Tradition also did—but that has shifted some—add weights.

Experience and reason and looking at the whole of Scriptures and Jesus' teachings lead us to add some weights against it.

The scales tip against Scripture in this case.

So, it's not so easy after all, is it, simply to say we take the Scriptures at face value. As United Methodists we have never been at our best when we reduced our positions to proof-texting. We need to be honest enough to say we do not *always* depend on a literal interpretation of Scripture for our final positions on many issues. For years, we used Scriptures effectively against women in ordained ministry and marrying divorced persons, as well as supporting slavery.

What we must conclude is that our understanding and interpretation of Scriptures is always partially distorted and always subject to review. If we can do this with integrity and humility, if we can do this with tears and honest struggle, we might have some healthy conversation about this issue and the many others that will follow.

In her compelling sermon at Simpsonwood Bishop Huie provided one of those warrants of experience Bishop Chamberlain mentioned.

Some time back, a pastor came to see me to talk about a situation in his congregation. A couple in his church has a new baby. They have wanted a child for years, didn't think they could have one, and now here she is—a beautiful baby girl. They want their pastor to baptize the baby. The couple is two women. "What should he do?" asked the pastor. We talked a while about a theology of baptism and God's grace and the church's covenant, and I said, "It seems to me you should baptize this child." "That's good," he said, "because I already did it." "My next question is this, her parents want me to bless the covenant they have made together. They also want their daughter to grow up in a home in which parents are bound for life in sacred covenant. What am I to do?"

I could feel something inside me shift. As much as I tried to keep it from happening, it happened anyway. When the pastor said, "bless the covenant they have made," I dropped the shepherd's staff. It just slipped out of my hands because I had to pick up the *Book of Discipline.* What began as a pastoral conversation turned into a legal conversation, a political conversation. I fulfilled my responsibility to obey the covenant I made at my consecration. While this pastor disagrees with the action of the General Conference, he too will stand within the covenant. Before he left my office, this pastor said to me, "Bishop, don't you see? Don't you see? This new restriction is keeping me from being shepherd to the flock where you appointed me." I was and am deeply disturbed by his statement.

Bishop Huie then explained why she has "great hope in this Council of Bishops—that we can talk here together about this issue and countless others that may be less divisive but more far-reaching." She told the bishops:

> The practice of prayer is drawing us together at a deeper level. We are spending more time in biblical and theological reflection about underlying issues. The practice of studying the Scriptures and doing theology together is knitting us together. . . . The practice of discernment is helping us to lay aside our individual wills and search for God's will, and it draws us together.

I do not suggest that these three bishops, much less their colleagues, are of one mind. But, increasingly, UMC bishops are of one spirit. They are beginning to provide strong spiritual leadership that will allow the church to hear and answer God's call.

A Vision of the Future

Where do we go from here? My surveys, interviews, observations, and conversations have made me hopeful about the future of the UMC. But no one knows the future. I offer this vision tentatively, inviting those who see the future differently to dialogue with me. Because I "see through a glass darkly," I offer this vision in the spirit of John Wesley and adopt as my own his words that began chapter 4:

> But some may say, I have mistaken the way myself, although I take upon me to teach it to others. It is probable many will think this, and it is very possible that I have. But I trust, whereinsoever I have mistaken, my mind is open to conviction. I sincerely desire to be better informed, I say to God and man, "What I know not, teach thou me! For God's sake, if it be possible to avoid it, let us not provoke one another to wrath. Let us not kindle in each other this fire of hell; much less blow it up into a flame. If we could discern truth by that dreadful light, would it not be loss, rather than gain? For, how far is love, even with many wrong opinions, to be preferred before truth itself without love!

Looking toward the future, I see leaders with strong biblical faith energizing United Methodists throughout the world. I see them connecting United Methodists with the power of the Bible, teaching them to view the Bible in its cultural context and to listen for the living word God speaks in our own time. I see these leaders in every nation and culture. I see these leaders at all levels—bishops, pastors, Sunday school teachers, and leaders of small groups. I see ordinary lay people leading as well (recall that the General Conference lay delegates are a bit more liberal in their approach to the Bible than the clergy delegates). A lay delegate who considers herself a religious conservative told me that problems on abortion and homosexuality "begin in local churches with pastors who do not support our belief to 'think and let think.' People are taught rigidity rather than the free flow of God's love." Spiritual leadership can occur at every level, and we can all learn from one another.

I see a new surge of United Methodist evangelism throughout the world. I see more institutional acceptance and support for conservatives, ministers, and lay people, who in personal evangelism seek out those best served by traditional means of evangelism. Yet, I see these conservatives applauding as more and more liberals, ministers and lay people, rise to the challenge of personal evangelism in terms that the liberals of modern cultures can understand—to be sure, a quite different type of evangelism. These words of Umphrey Lee, a former president of Southern Methodist University, written more than fifty years ago still ring true:

> I see a new surge of United Methodist evangelism.

> Wesley was proposing a communion of Christians based upon a positive theological doctrine: the doctrine that few doctrines are essential. . . . It does not seem that in our day there has been much choice for those who would pursue an active evangelical Christian life but who object to weighty fetters of doctrine or of worship. It may be that now there is a peculiar place for Wesley's comprehension, when the Word of Life must be reinterpreted to a generation that knows it not. . . . [Tolerance] in all that does not interfere with the love of God and the work of divine grace is a good principle for the twentieth century [and the twenty-first!],

as it was for the eighteenth; and against the narrowing tendencies of our present controversies The [United] Methodist Church had better keep alive her ancient glory, "a glorifying peculiar to us," that we think and let think.[14]

I see such evangelism directed at christianizing not just individuals but also the social structures that impinge on their lives. Both traditional and contemporary approaches to evangelism can be authentically Wesleyan. With both approaches I see us all heeding W. E. Sangster's plea "for personal evangelism led by the minister of every Methodist church and heartily sustained by [the] people." Sangster warns that personal evangelism "may mean another journey to the Cross. It may mean the most rigid self-examination to discover if there is some individual problem filching our power to serve, and it must work itself out first in the church. The fellowship must be rich enough and warm enough to nourish the life of those new-born in Christ." Yet the results of such evangelism are startling. Let the minister seek Christ's

> guidance concerning the one person to whom [that minister] is to turn with his witness, and let him prove his gospel in one life. . . . To see one life revolutionized by Jesus would revolutionize the service of some despairing [pastors]. It would revolutionize the local church. It is amazing how large a small congregation looks when it includes the shining faces of new disciples, and the enheartenment it gives to the whole church can hardly be exaggerated.[15]

I see us focusing not just on telling the gospel story in traditional and modern terms but also on showing that story in our ministry to the world. Jesus taught us that God's focus is on the world. "God loved the world so much that he gave his only Son, that everyone who has faith in him may

I see us showing the gospel story in our ministry to the world.

not die but have eternal life." Several United Methodist leaders have reminded us of this focus. Though Bishop Kenneth L. Carder may understate the need to face the crisis within the church, he certainly puts this crisis in biblical perspective when he says:

> Thirty-five thousand children dying every day from malnutrition and hunger, when Jesus warned that harming one child is an invitation to judgment: That is a crisis! Forty million people perishing each year from poverty-related causes, when Jesus said he came to bring good news to the poor: that is a crisis! Millions of people being pushed to the margins of society and denied their full dignity as children of God because of the color of their skin, when God shows no partiality: That is a crisis![16]

Bishop Ray Owen, in his helpful book, *The Witness We Make: To Heal Our Dividedness*[17] sees the Bishops' Initiative on Children and Poverty as a compelling force for unity of the church and a sign of hope for the future of the UMC. I see us gathering people at the Bible to receive the power of God for our efforts to resolve the problems of children in poverty, world peace, and health care; for championing the civil rights of all people; for calling people to fidelity in relationships; for taking the Bible away from political extremists; and for understanding the Bible in its cultural and historical context.

I see our mission focus putting the homosexuality issue in perspective. Many delegates think this issue is getting in the way of higher priorities. Many readers will sympathize with the delegate who wrote on the back of the questionnaire, "I regret that this document spent half its space on two social issues, abortion and homosexuality. So many more issues were so much more important—ministry, baptism, ecumenism, mission." Tony Campolo reminds us that homosexuality was not on Jesus' list of concerns. One professor I know told his class that "someone from outer space reading the Bible to find out how to be a disciple would far more likely become concerned about poverty and health care than about what people do in bed." Speaking of the Initiative on Children and Poverty, Bishop Peter Storey of the Methodist Church of Southern Africa said:

> Isn't it wonderful that, because of this initiative to children in poverty, instead of fretting about membership loss you can now become passionately concerned about the loss of little lives? . . . Isn't it wonderful that instead of expending massive emotional energy debating whether you can be gay and Christian—about which Scripture has virtually nothing understandable to say—God gives you the chance to find out whether you can be rich and Christian—a far more serious question?[18]

Our collective declaration that homosexual persons are of equal worth and the resulting affirmation of their civil rights is already an important contribution to the resolution of the public issue of homosexuality in the U.S. and abroad. In the near future I see increasing numbers of United Methodist churches agreeing that homosexual persons are of equal worth before God, championing their civil rights, and making public expressions of support and acceptance. As a way of witnessing to the community, our pastor, for example, used the mother's testimony described above as the basis of a one-minute radio spot.

I see more studies such as those inspired by the Committee on Homosexuality as well as more dialogues such as those initiated by the UMC General Commission on Christian Unity and Interreligious Concerns. Such studies and dialogues are powerful venues for opening our minds and enlarging our circles of friends. And they will foster in all our conferencing the kind of discernment called for by the Committee on Plan of Organization and

Rules of the 2000 General Conference which envisioned: "times, in the midst of deliberation, when we will need to stop, pray together, listen in silence together, and refocus our common vision of where the spirit is leading the church."[19]

As we persuade our members to accept the positions we have already agreed on and persuade our churches to make these agreements visible to their communities, we will sharpen our witness to God at work in the world. As time goes by I see us going further. I see most United Methodists determined to avoid a schism that will diminish our capacity to make disciples of Christ and to participate powerfully in God's redemption of our societies and cultures. More positively, I see United Methodists, wherever we are on the continuum of views on homosexuality issues, recognizing our spiritual common ground. I see us fashioning creative agreements that will allow us to live our lives and missions together under the guidance of the Holy Spirit. I see the large reservoir of civility among United Methodists and the signs of spiritual awakening like those discussed above emboldening our leaders throughout the world and at all levels of the church. Already I have found liberals beginning to pay more attention to biblical morality. Some of our most liberal bishops are talking about making disciples and about spiritual leadership. I see this as only the first fruits of the work of the Holy Spirit among the liberals. Conservatives and their caucuses played an important role in bringing a new spiritual awakening. I see them being open to the leading of the Holy Spirit—standing by biblical morality—but being open to a more complex view. Already I have found a few conservatives recognizing that pastoral discretion on celebration of same-sex unions may be acceptable some day.

> Most United Methodists want to avoid a schism which will diminish our capacity to make disciples of Jesus Christ.

As we continue talking about the Bible, I see us eventually simply acknowledging that, while we do agree on homosexuals' worth and on their rights, we simply do not agree on whether there might be some homosexual practice that is compatible with biblical teaching. This lack of agreement is evident in the votes of the General Conferences discussed above, in the participation of more than 150 United Methodist clergy in the celebration of the "holy union" of two women in Sacramento, and, more recently, in the contrasting actions on this issue at the 1999 annual conferences.[20] I see us agreeing that promiscuous and/or exploitative homosexual relations like promiscuous and/or exploitative heterosexual relations are *not* compatible with Christian teaching. Yet I see us acknowledging that we are not of one mind on whether responsible, committed, same-sex unions may meet the test of biblical morality. At the same time, with enhanced awareness of the role of culture in mediating God's revelation and widening experience of the Holy Spirit working in the lives of such couples, I see increasing numbers of Methodists agreeing that such same-sex unions can meet that test. Just as important, I see those who do not agree about same-sex unions recognizing that those who celebrate them are sincere biblical Christians who acknowledge the authority of the Scriptures and experience its power.

As a clear distinction between "marriage" and "holy union" emerges, I see the issue of celebrating same-sex unions being worked out eventually—initially at the local level. Wesley believed strongly that each Christian is

united by the tenderest and closest ties to one particular congregation. There he partakes of all the ordinances of God. There he receives the supper of the Lord. There he pours out his soul in public prayer, and joins in public praise and thanksgiving. There he rejoices to hear the word of reconciliation, the gospel of the grace of God. With these his nearest, his best-beloved brethren, on solemn occasions, he seeks God by fasting. These particularly he watches over in love, as they do over his soul; admonishing, exhorting, comforting, reproving, and every way building up each other in the faith. These he regards as his own household; and therefore, according to the ability God has given him, naturally cares for them, and provides that they may have all the things that are needful for life and godliness.[21]

In this context I see United Methodist lay people who sincerely believe that some same-sex unions meet the test of biblical morality quietly celebrating gay and lesbian couples' commitments in their homes or other settings outside church buildings. This way they would accept the commitments of their United Methodist brothers and sisters yet honor the agreements we have made in the General Conference. Moreover, many congregations would not object to a pastor praying with any couple about their commitment to one another. Eventually, I see us allowing pastoral discretion whether to celebrate such unions.[22] Most Methodists would likely oppose this now and in the near future, but recall that 38 percent of U.S. delegates to the 1996 General Conference already voted against prohibiting such celebrations. Wherever we are on this issue, it is important for all of us to understand that those who want permission to celebrate holy unions are not rejecting biblical morality. These clergy are asking a fair question: "If sex is God's good gift and God has made many homosexuals the way they are, are we right to deny them recognition of their committed relationships?" Granting pastoral discretion will not open the floodgates—look at what a strong statement the *Discipline* makes about marriage. I see pastors setting forth the same high standards of loyalty and commitment to same-sex couples, calling them to a "covenant that is expressed in love, mutual support, personal commitment, and shared fidelity."

Still further on the horizon I see some flexibility on the ordination issue as well, beginning, perhaps, by our removing the proscriptions that refer specifically to homosexuality but more rigorously applying the remaining criteria for ordination. Eventually this change would likely lead to some ordinations of gay and lesbian candidates who are in unions that, in the judgment of the appropriate committees, pass the test of biblical morality. Where such ordinations occur, initially I see many congregations refusing to accept a gay man or lesbian as their pastor, but in the appointment process the District Superintendent already is mandated to take into account "the convictional stance of the congregation: theology; prejudices if any; spiritual life. . . ."

Emerging Agreements

In reaching new agreements on homosexuality and in enforcing them, I see us heeding the apostle Paul's counsel to put Christ's love first. This may mean making some allowances for the slower pace at which communal customs are changing, not only in some local communities in the United States but also within whole societies served by the global church. Putting Christ's love first will not immediately resolve our differences, but it will sustain our unity.

> Putting Christ's love first means making some allowances for the slower pace of cultural change in some communities and societies.

A Cloud of Witnesses

In short, I do envision a vibrant United Methodist Church united on the essentials of the faith. I see a church claiming its rich heritage and waking to God's call. I see a church shaping history by leading contemporary people and societies to a culturally aware, biblical faith. I see a church showing the world the power of that faith. I know full well that this vision is of "a morrow which the mere passage of time will not make to dawn" (Thoreau). But, if we keep on talking about the Bible, opening our minds, enlarging our circles, and honoring our agreements, the dawn will come! We affirm the authority of the Bible that shows us God at work in the world. The God of the Bible—the God of Abraham, Isaac, and Jacob; the God of Miriam and Sarah and Ruth; the God of Peter and Paul; the God and Father of our Lord Jesus Christ will not be contained in the Bible. God will not be limited by the limitations of the people in the times and cultures of the Bible. Believing this frees us to open our minds as we watch together for God's authentic, contemporary word—discerning where the Spirit leads.

Sometimes we will watch passively in prayer, as Jesus wanted his disciples to do in Gethsemane. The United Methodist bishops formed a continuous prayer vigil at the 1996 General Conference and invited everyone to participate. Various United Methodist groups throughout the world were also in continuous prayer for the conference. Many have called United Methodists to pray specifically for the UMC in its present crisis. For example, the 1998 Confessing Movement conference invited "all United Methodists to engage in fasting and in regular, intentional prayer for the renewal of The United Methodist Church." Through such prayer we may discern what God is doing in our world.

Often there is need for watchful action in which, as we become alert to what God is doing, our actions become instruments of divine purpose. The 1992 General Conference's commitment to champion basic rights and liberties for homosexual persons was such an action. Paul earnestly urged the Christians in Corinth, "Keep alert, stand firm in your faith, be courageous, be strong. Let all that you do be done in love" (1 Corinthians 16:13-14). In that spirit we can bring the truth and power of the Bible into the lives of contemporary people and societies.

We do not watch alone. In Sunday worship the morning after I returned from observing the Theological Diversity Dialogues in Dallas, we sang "The Church's One Foundation." During the third verse my wife looked at me and smiled. Looking back at the words "by schisms rent asunder" I was surprised. Surely she knows that the more United Methodists I talk with across the country, the more enthusiastic I become about the future of the UMC. After the service she responded to my expression of surprise: "No, no it was the next line: 'yet saints their watch are keeping.'"

God's church transcends us! We are surrounded by "so great a cloud of witnesses" from every age and culture (Hebrews 12:1). They watch with us as we each tell the gospel story in ways our culture can understand—and as we show the impact of that story on our lives.

NOTES

Introduction

1. A few weeks after the 1996 General Conference ended, I surveyed the U.S. delegates by mail. Each delegate received an eighty-four item questionnaire. Most of the items asked delegates to circle a response indicating the extent of their agreement or disagreement with the statement presented (for example, "The UMC has become too diverse."); but about 20 percent of the questionnaire gave them a chance to set down their reflections on the General Conference in a more open fashion (for example, "Can you think of a common ground position that might lead to a resolution of the homosexuality issue? If so, briefly describe that position."). Five hundred and eighty-nine delegates (70 percent of the U.S. delegates) returned completed questionnaires. Those who did not respond are quite similar to those who did on gender, geographical location, lay or clergy status, and legislative committee assignments. This similarity suggests that the responses I received are indeed representative of the U.S. delegates to the General Conference. Unfortunately, for practical reasons (such as the difficulty of translating questionnaires and responses, cost of foreign postage, and expected mail delays) I did not include the almost 200 international delegates.

2. Davis, James Allan and Tom W. Smith: General Social Surveys, 1972–1996 [machine-readable data file]. Principal Investigator, James A. Davis; Director and Co-Principal Investigator, Tom W. Smith. NORC, ed. Chicago: National Opinion Research Center, producer, 1996; Storrs, Conn.: The Roper Center for Public Opinion Research, University of Connecticut, distributor. 1 data file (35,284 logical records) and 1 codebook (1295 pp.). I was also able to obtain preliminary data from the 1998 poll.

Chapter 1. Seeing Our Differences

1. A good history of the UMC's struggle with homosexuality issues is included in *The Church Studies Homosexuality* (Nashville: Cokesbury, 1994).

2. _1996 The United Methodist Church General Conference Daily Christian Advocate_, III, no. 7: 284.

3. _The Book of Discipline of the United Methodist Church, 1996_ (Nashville: The United Methodist Publishing House, 1996), ¶ 65G, 89.

4. _1996 Daily Christian Advocate_, Advance Edition, II: 1217.

5. _United Methodist News Service_, 9 March 1999 and 13 April 1999.

6. _The Book of Discipline, 1996_, ¶ 65G, 87. Since we will see in chapter 6 that this action did not resolve the issue, it should be noted here that the General Conference debated whether it would be appropriate to place this statement in the Social Principles, which have usually been regarded as instructive and hortatory rather than binding legislation. When the General Conference referred the matter to the Judicial Council it responded: "This is a legislative placement decision. We do not have jurisdiction." It is fair to say that most delegates who wanted to prohibit "ceremonies that celebrate homosexual unions" understood this ruling to mean that binding legislation could be placed within the Social Principles. Still, one only needs to read the Preface to the Social Principles to understand why the Judicial Council would have to revisit this issue two years later. For example, the Preface contains the sentence: "[The Social Principles] are intended to be instructive and persuasive in the best of the prophetic spirit. The Social Principles are a call to all members of The United Methodist Church to a prayerful, studied dialogue of faith and practice" (p. 84).

7. _The Book of Discipline, 1996_, ¶ 304i2, 172.

8. _Good News_ (May / June 1998).

9. "Open Letter to the Council of Bishops," paid advertisement in _The United Methodist Reporter_ (19 February 1999).

10. _The Book of Discipline, 1996_, ¶ 65J, 90.

11. Lydia Saad, "Americans Growing More Tolerant of Gays" _The Gallup Poll: Public Releases from Gallup Poll Results_ (14 December 1996).

12. "The New South and the New Baptists" _Christian Century_ 103 (14 May 1986): 486-88.

13. _The United Methodist Reporter_, 11 July 1997.

14. _The Biblical Doctrine of Election_ (London: Lutterworth Press, 1953), 94.

15. Umphrey Lee, "Freedom from Rigid Creed," in _Methodism_, ed. William K. Anderson (Nashville: The Methodist Publishing House, 1947), 129.

16. Lee, "Freedom from Rigid Creed," 128.

17. _The Works of John Wesley_ (Grand Rapids, Mich., Zondervan Publishing House [1872]), vol. V, 498-99.

18. _The Works of John Wesley_, vol. V, 500-501.

19. Daniel V. A. Olson and William McKinney, "United Methodist Leaders: Diversity and Moral Authority," in *The People(s) Called Methodist*, ed. William B. Lawrence, Dennis M. Campbell, and Russell E. Richey (Nashville: Abingdon Press, 1998), 120.

Chapter 2. Claiming Our Heritage

1. *1996 Daily Christian Advocate* III, no. 2: 1.

2. *The Book of Discipline*, 1996 ¶ 509, 277.

3. Paul A. Mickey and Robert L. Wilson, *What New Creation?* (Nashville: Abingdon, 1977), 128.

4. Ibid.

5. *The Journal of the Reverend John Wesley* (New York: E. P. Dutton & Company, 1915), vol. 2, 499.

6. Most of the percentages reported in this chapter are based on the following two open-ended questions. Percentages may sum to more than 100 because some delegates listed, for example, two high points of the conference. Before influencing delegates by specific questions, I wanted to hear what impressed them most at the General Conference. The first question of the survey was the following open-ended question. Q1 "Considering everything, what stands out as the high point of the 1996 General Conference for you?" Toward the end of the questionnaire, I asked another open-ended question. Q71 "What action or event, if any, of the 1996 General Conference most contributed to strengthening the sense of community of United Methodists?"

7. I will frequently refer to delegates as "conservative" or "liberal" based on their responses to the following survey question: Question 79. "In religious matters, would you describe yourself as: (Please circle one number) 1 Very Conservative, 2 Conservative, 3 Liberal, 4 Very Liberal." Two or 3 delegates rebelled against such labels, and several wrote in "moderate." However, most delegates, as most Americans, apparently had little difficulty with labeling themselves.

8. *1996 Daily Christian Advocate*, III, no. 2: 22.

9. Lee, "Freedom from Rigid Creed," 128.

10. *The Works of John Wesley*, vol. V, 499.

11. *The Works of John Wesley* vol. V, 498-501.

12. Additional responses included approval of ministry study (5 percent); positive experience in legislative committees (3 percent); the Episcopal Address (3 percent); and the fifteen bishops' statement on homosexuality (13 delegates—2.5 percent of the total mentioned this as a positive high point; 3 delegates—.5 percent of the total mentioned it as

a negative high point). Other mentions by at least five delegates: Giving more flexibility to Annual Conference structure (10 delegates); maintaining positions on homosexuality or rejecting more liberal positions (9 delegates); and diversity of membership (8 delegates).

13. Olson and McKinney, "United Methodist Leaders," 110, 126.

14. *1996 Daily Christian Advocate*, Advance Edition, I: 171.

15. *1996 Daily Christian Advocate*, III, no. 10: 693.

16. *1996 Daily Christian Advocate*, III, no. 2: 20.

17. *The Journal of the Reverend John Wesley* (New York: E. P. Dutton & Company, 1913), vol. 1, 8.

18. See Walter G. Muelder, "Methodism's Contribution to Social Reform," in *Methodism*, ed. William K. Anderson (Nashville: The Methodist Publishing House, 1947), 194-204.

19. Walter Rauschenbusch, *The Righteousness of the Kingdom* (Nashville: Abingdon Press, 1968), 102-103.

20. *1996 Daily Christian Advocate*, III, no. 10: 655.

Chapter 3. Talking About the Bible

1. William M. Easum, *Sacred Cows Make Gourmet Burgers: Ministry Anytime, Anywhere, by Anybody* (Nashville: Abingdon Press, 1995), 8.

2. G. Ernest Wright, *God Who Acts* (London: SCM Press, 1952), 12.

3. *The Book of Discipline, 1996*, ¶ 63, 75-76.

4. *In Search of Unity: A Conversation with Recommendations for the Unity of The United Methodist Church* (New York: General Commission on Christian Unity and Interreligious Concerns, 1998), 5.

5. *Merriam Webster's Collegiate Dictionary* (Springfield, Massachusetts: Merriam-Webster, Incorporated, 1997), 282. This dictionary definition captures the social science meaning of the concept of culture.

6. *The Book of Discipline, 1996*, ¶ 63, 76.

7. I admire the scholarly work of Richard B. Hays, and recommend his book *The Moral Vision of the New Testament: A Contemporary Introduction to New Testament Ethics* (San Francisco: HarperSanFrancisco, 1996). However, I fail to see how his treatment of the issue of homosexuality is consistent with his apparent awareness of the role of culture in mediating God's revelation.

8. Thomas Edward Frank, *Polity, Practice, and the Mission of The United Methodist Church* (Nashville: Abingdon Press, 1997), 90.

9. *The Works of John Wesley* (Grand Rapids, Michigan: Zondervan Publishing House ([1872]), vol. V, 497.

10. *1996 Daily Christian Advocate*, III, no. 10: 684.

11. H. Richard Niebuhr, *Christ and Culture* (New York: Harper & Brothers Publishers, 1951), 39-40.

Chapter 4. Opening Our Minds

1. *The Works of John Wesley*, vol. V, 5.

2. Mark A. Noll, *The Scandal of the Evangelical Mind* (Grand Rapids, Mich.: William B. Eerdmans Publishing, 1994), 141.

3. Noll, *The Scandal of the Evangelical Mind*, 136-137.

4. Ibid., 136.

5. *United Methodist News Service*, 13 May 1998.

6. Craig Calhoun, ed., *Habermas and the Public Sphere* (Cambridge, Massachusetts: The MIT Press, 1992), 13.

7. *The Book of Discipline, 1996*, ¶ 65G, 88-89.

8. Noll, *The Scandal of the Evangelical Mind*, 51.

9. *The Book of Resolutions of The United Methodist Church, 1996* (Nashville: The United Methodist Publishing House, 1996), 33.

10. Spencer A. Rathus, Jeffrey S. Nevid, and Lois Fichner-Rathus, *Human Sexuality in a World of Diversity* (Boston: Allyn and Bacon, 1997), 282.

11. Rathus, Nevid, and Fichner-Rathus, *Human Sexuality*, 283.

12. Saad, "More Tolerant of Gays."

13. *Emerging Trends* (December 1997): 5.

14. Rathus, Nevid, and Fichner-Rathus, *Human Sexuality*, 276.

15. John Bancroft, "Problematic Gender Identity and Sexual Orientation: A Psychiatrist's View," in *Sex and Gender: A Theological and Scientific Inquiry*, ed. Mark. F. Schwartz et al. (St. Louis, Mo.: The Pope John Center, 1983), 102-24.

16. Jeanne Knepper and Morris Floyd, "By Any Other Name," *AFFIRM!* 13 (April 1996): 2.

17. James Davison Hunter, *Culture Wars: The Struggle to Define America* (New York: BasicBooks, 1991), 44.

18. David Head, *He Sent Leanness: A Book of Prayers for the Natural Man* (New York: The Macmillan Company, 1959), 14.

19. *The Book of Resolutions, 1996*, 242-43.

20. Noll, *The Scandal of the Evangelical Mind*, 115.

21. *1996 Daily Christian Advocate*, III, no. 3: 63.

Chapter 5. Enlarging Our Circles

1. James S. Coleman, *Community Conflict* (Glencoe, Ill.: Free Press, 1957), 22.

2. Data on congregations from a major study being conducted by Nancy T. Ammerman, Adair Lummis, and David Roozen at Hartford Seminary, suggests that the contrast between the Western and Southeastern Jurisdictions on attitudes toward homosexuality exists at

the congregational level as well as at the level of General Conference delegates.

3. N. J. Demerath, *Social Class in American Protestantism* (Chicago: Rand McNally, 1965).

4. Wade Clark Roof and William McKinney, *American Mainline Reli-- gion: Its Changing Shape of the Religious Establishment* (New Brunswick, N.J.: Rutgers University Press, 1987).

5. For comparison, 68 percent of a national sample disapprove *legally sanctioned* gay marriage, while 27 percent approve (*Emerging Trends*, April 1996). It is possible, of course, that some delegates would make a clear distinction between legally sanctioned marriage and church sanctioned marriage.

6. Russell E. Richey, *The Methodist Conference in America: A History* (Nashville: Kingswood Books, 1996), 204.

7. Lyle E. Schaller, "Is Schism the Next Step?" *Circuit Rider*, (September/October, 1998), 4-5.

Chapter 6. Honoring Our Agreements

1. *UM News Service*, 25 March 1998

2. *UM News Service*, 15 March 1999. See also "Debate Over Same-Sex Marriage Splits a Methodist Church Near Atlanta," *The New York Times*, 24 June 1999, A 19.

3. *1996 Daily Christian Advocate, Advance Edition*, I: 170.

4. Staff memo to "All Editors of Curriculum Materials," 12 March 1962.

5. *1992 Daily Christian Advocate*, IV, no. 4: 185.

6. See also the *United Methodist News Service* account of the demonstration, 28 April 1998.

7. *United Methodist News Service*, 23 March 1999. For a forceful statement that bishops should not voice their disagreement with church law, see John Ed Mathison, William Bauknight, and Mary Daffin (Officers of the Confessing Movement within The UMC), "We are alarmed by clergy support of same-sex unions," *The United Methodist Reporter*, 13 November 1998, 4.

Chapter 7. A Time to Lead

1. Alfred North Whitehead, *Adventure of Ideas* (New York: Macmillan Company, 1952), 23.

2. Whitehead, *Adventures of Ideas*, 26, 28.

3. *Emerging Trends* (April, 1996).

4. For example, many Republicans have expressed concern that, in

addressing homosexuality issues, some of their leaders have used the Bible in a way that obscures the complexity of the issues. See Richard L. Berke, "Intraparty Debate Breaks Out Among Republicans over Criticism of Gays," *The New York Times,* 30 June 1998.

5. Letha D. Scanzoni and Virginia R. Mollenkott, *Is the Homosexual My Neighbor? Another Christian View* (New York: HarperSanFrancisco, 1980).

6. James Allen Davis and Tom W. Smith, *General Social Surveys, 1972-1998* [machine-readable data file] (Chicago: National Opinion Research Center, 1998).

7. The intent of this discussion is to highlight the way the early church gave priority to the gifts of the Holy Spirit rather than to the laws of their Jewish heritage. Peter recognized this priority as he considered whether there should be a distinction between Jews and non-Jews. The early church's sense of priority sets an important precedent for us today as we consider whether some homosexual unions pass the test of biblical morality—hence may be blessed by the church. In this case, of course, we are not considering Christians and non-Christians. These homosexual persons are United Methodist Christians, members of our congregations. (It is true that the 1972 General Conference received large numbers of petitions to exclude practicing homosexuals from membership in The United Methodist Church, but the General Conference took no such action. Most United Methodists today agree with the General Conference's wisdom.)

8. *The United Methodist Reporter,* 3 April 1998, 2.

9. John Selby Spong, "Anglicans Get Literal," *The New York Times,* 13 August 1998, A23.

10. Cynthia B. Astle, "A Good Model for Handling Church Conflict," *The United Methodist Reporter,* 138, no. 16 {13 September 1991): 2.

11. David Owen, *Getting There From Here* (Bloomington, Ind.: St. Mark's United Methodist Church, 1995), 16-17.

12. Janis Thornton, "Indy Pastor Moderates 'Healing Dialogue' at Nebraska Annual Conference," *Hoosier United Methodist News,* (July/August 1998): 15.

13. *Newscope* 26, no. 28 (10 July 1998).

14. Lee, "Freedom from Rigid Creed," 137-38.

15. W. E. Sangster, *Methodism Can Be Born Again* (New York: The Methodist Book Concern, 1938), 98-100.

16. "Crisis Talk May Be the Crisis," *United Methodist News Service,* 15 April 1998.

17. Ray Owen, *The Witness We Make: To Heal Our Dividedness* (Nashville: Abingdon Press, 1998).

18. *The United Methodist Reporter,* 3 July 1998, 2.

19. *UM News Service,* 15 June 1999.

20. At least 20 annual conference sessions adopted petitions or resolutions for maintaining or strengthening the *Discipline's* restrictions related to homosexuality. In contrast, at least seven annual conference sessions took actions aimed at making the church more accepting of homosexual persons (*UM News Service,* 30 June 1999). The most dramatic action related to the matter of same-sex unions was the Northern Illinois Annual Conference's election of the Reverend Greg Dell as a delegate to the 2000 General Conference. In March 1999 a church trial convicted Dell for performing a same-sex union (*UM News Service,* 10 June 1999). In September 1999 the North Central Jurisdiction Committee on Appeals upheld Dell's suspension, fixing the period from July 5, 1999, to June 30, 2000. A pastor under suspension cannot be seated as a General Conference delegate (*United Methodist News Service,* 20 September 1999). Lack of agreement was further evidenced by the performance of another service of holy union by the Reverend Jimmy Creech in April 1999, leading to a second trial for him (*United Methodist News Service,* 24 September 1999).

21. *The Works of John Wesley,* vol. V, 502-03.

22. Retired United Methodist Bishop Jack Tuell asked delegates to the 2000 General Conference to re-affirm "the centrality and uniqueness of marriage between a man and a woman," but to repeal the policy that prohibits United Methodist clergy from conducting ceremonies that celebrate homosexual unions. Bishop Tuell, who was the presiding judge in the trial that convicted the Reverend Greg Dell, believes that "United Methodist ministers who are appointed to a variety of situations should have the right to determine the spiritual and pastoral needs of people whom they serve." The freedom and integrity of pastors was one of seven reasons for dropping the prohibition that Bishop Tuell listed in his letter to about 60 General Conference delegates: "The issue in this matter has to do with the freedom and integrity of our clergy to carry out their ministry in the place where they are appointed. It is not primarily on whether you are for or against changing the present general position of the UMC regarding homosexuality. Persons on either side of this larger issue should see the unfairness and injustice of sending our ministers out to serve all the people and then throwing them out when they try to do so" (*United Methodist News Service,* 5 October 1999).